LUND STUDIES IN GEOGRAPHY 56

Ground Level Development

NGOs, Co-operatives and Local Organizations
in the Third World

Editors: Hans Holmén and Magnus Jirström

Lund
University
Press

Lund University Press
Box 141
S-221 00 Lund
Sweden

© 1994 Hans Holmén and Magnus Jirström (eds)

Art nr 20347
ISSN 1400-1144
ISBN 91-7966-295-1 Lund University Press
ISBN 0-86238-379-X Chartwell-Bratt

Printed in Sweden
Studentlitteratur
Lund 1994

Contents

PREFACE 5

CHAPTER ONE 7
OLD WINE IN NEW BOTTLES? - Local organizations as Panacea for Sustainable Development.
By Hans Holmén and Magnus Jirström

CHAPTER TWO 37
CO-OPERATIVES AND THE ENVIRONMENTAL CHALLENGE - What Can Local Organizations Do?
By Hans Holmén

CHAPTER THREE 63
CO-OPERATIVES AS INSTRUMENT OF RURAL DEVELOPMENT - The Case of India.
By Neelambar Hatti and Franz-Michael Rundquist

CHAPTER FOUR 83
WHY IS LOCAL PARTICIPATION SO WEAK?
Twenty-fife Years of Institution Building in Muda, Malaysia.
By Magnus Jirström

CHAPTER FIVE 108
AGRO-INDUSTRIES, CO-OPERATIVES AND RURAL DEVELOPMENT IN THE PHILIPPINES
By Esteban Pagaran

POST SCRIPTUM 137
By Hans Holmén and Magnus Jirström

Preface

This anthology adresses a complex theme: Local organizations (LOs) in the development process. The study-field embraces a number of important questions: How can people be organized at local level in a manner that simultaneously (a) spreads incentives and benefits so as to allow more people, especially the poor and remotely situated, to be positively involved in the development process; (b) builds on local knowledge and practices while at the same time enhancing the necessary spread of innovations (material and immaterial); and, most important, (c) does this in a sustainable manner, *viz.* that the local organization neither collapses once the initial support period is over, nor threatens the physical resource base on which we all depend. Needless to say, we do not attempt to present the ultimate answers to these questions. But it is our intention to contribute to a better appreciation of matters involved.

The theme of organization has gained renewed attention in recent years. Particularly the role(s) of and expectations on various local, non-governmental as well as formal and informal (pre-) co-operative organizations in the Third World has been a matter of much controversy. Moreover, it is often not clear what is meant by these various labels. Consequently, we need more empirically based information in order to arrive at a realistic assessment of the potential(s) and limitations of Third World local organizations as development instruments.

This book represents a first step towards that end. It contains both theoretical and conceptual discussions on the one hand, and reports from field-research on the other. All research is done within the framework of the research programme *Co-operatives and Local Organizations in Rural Development*, Department for Social and Economic Geography, University of Lund, Sweden. Next on the groups agenda is a broad-based, systematic inventory of LO performance in various parts of the Third world. Only with the help of such an inventory may we allow ourselves to generalize about LOs in the development process.

Organization of the Book

In the introductory chapter, *Hans Holmén* and *Magnus Jirström* make the outline for the main theme of this book - local organizations and their role in rural development. The emphasis is laid on how organizations under different labels have been designated as solutions to problems in rural development during the post-colonial era. Holmén and Jirström also develop the framework for some central concepts used in this book, concepts with particular relevance to the potential of organizations for development purposes in a long-term perspective.

Hans Holmén (chapter two) analyses the potential role of Local Organizations in environmental protection. Using co-operative organizations as examples, the author compares expectations about what these organizations could achieve as developemnts instruments with empirical observations about what has actually been achieved.

In the third chapter *Neelambar Hatti* and *Franz-Michael Rundquist* focus on organizational barriers that influence the room in which local organizations operate. Their paper analyzes the environment of local and co-operative organizations in terms of different layers, notably the controlled, the influenceable and the appreciated environments which local organizations are confronted with, and the extent to which these are locally manipulable.

Magnus Jirström (chapter four) points at the need to establish local organizations in order to control crop pests and weeds in irrigated intensive cultivation. His paper discusses the reasons for the paradoxical absence of locally based farmers' organizations in a favoured rice-cultivating district in Malaysia where 'organizational support' has been massive for about twenty years.

In the final chapter, *Esteban Pagaran* describes the establishment of a tomato growers' producer co-operative as a consequence of agro-industry decentralization in the Philippines. His paper also discusses the effects on farmers' employment and income generation in comparison with similar production organized as direct company cultivation and private outgrower schemes.

Chapter One

Old Wine in New Bottles?

Local Organizations as Panacea for Sustainable Development

By Hans Holmén and Magnus Jirström.

Introduction

Both aid giving for developmental purposes and much, maybe most, research about 'development' tend to be rather interventionistic undertakings. This is often the case also when 'learning' is the stated objective. After all, "the fundamental motive for the study of less developed countries is to provide explanations for their poor economic performance *as this allows for the provision of policy guides for future development"* (Gunnarsson & Holmén 1994:36). This urge to intervene and change, while often praiseworthy as such, is, however, not without its pitfalls. It may be worth reminding that 'the road to hell is paved with good intentions'. This is especially so when efforts are made to present guide-lines with assumed general applicability.

Development -- and promotion of development -- is not only a complex but also a highly controversial matter. There sometimes seems to be as many definitions of development as there are writers about it. But that is not all. As pointed out by Hettne (1992:4), "people tend to disagree on the meaning of development, as soon as an effort to define it is made". Ideally, research about development should solve this problem by presenting better analyses of the matter. The fulfilment of such objectives, however, is mitigated by a number of factors. One is that, whichever definition of development we adopt, there are, most probably, a number of ways to achieve it.

In a highly varied world with a plethora of insufficiently understood local preconditions and (more or less) general influences, it is extremely difficult to find general recipies for poverty alleviation and development promotion. More analysis and a flexible understanding of development, therefore, seem to be required if aid giving and development promotion are to have the desired results in all different parts of the world.

However, development research, generally, is highly normative. Sometimes it is even declared that it must be normative (Hesselberg 1985; Lund 1986). In spite of the above mentioned need for a better understanding of the process(es) of development, many (most?) researchers and donors attracted to the field "want to change the world, not only analyse it" (Hettne 1992:2). This impatience, while quite understandable, we believe, often tends to lead to premature conclusions and, primarily, it seems recurringly to lead to the presentation of standard solutions to the problems of underdevelopment. This search for a development panacea, however, seems rather futile. It may help some writers to sell books -- but does it help the world's poor?

We do not attempt here to present a definition of 'development' that all can agree on. For reasons mentioned above, that seems rather impossible. But we believe that most people can agree that no matter how development is defined, it is to a large degree a matter of organization. During the last couple of decades, the question of how to (best) organize people - particularly poor people - in the Third World for 'developmental' purposes has been a persistent headache among Western aid and 'development' promotors. The latest fashion is to propagate the support of local (LO) and non-governmental (NGO) organizations in various parts of the Third World's rural areas. This allegedly "new" approach is believed to be superior to common practice which, generally, has emphasized the role of experts and governments in development projects.

Today, while everybody seems to advocate NGOs as the ultimate development instrument, there is also a great deal of disagreement and confusion both about what LOs and NGOs are and about what they can achieve. Hence, we presently find both right-wing and left-wing western proponents of LOs and NGOs advocating these organizations as either reformist or revolutionary forces in societal reorganization (Gutto 1993). However, to the extent that support to, or creation of, local organizations is presented as a panacea for development, there is reason for caution. Schmale (1993:2) stresses that "the strategy of supporting NGOs and LOs has yet to prove its effectiveness in making a major contribution towards the eradication of underdevelopment". For one thing, it is often unclear whether proponents of NGOs talk about NGOs having their base in industrialized countries (*i.e.* as alternative channels for aid money) or about NGOs in the Third World (*i.e.* as receivers of aid and/or independently evolved). Moreover, we still know too little about which indigenous local organizations there actually are to support in the Third World. Neither do we have sufficient understanding of their driving forces, nor about their abilities to contribute to development in general and poverty alleviation in particular. As a matter of fact,

> "The potential of local organizations is often overestimated. The number of successful NGO stories referred to in development literature is relatively small. A few cases such as the Grameen Bank in Bangladesh are repeated again and again" (*ibid*. p12).

There are many different kinds of local organizations in the Third World. Some are public like, for example, village or small town councils. Others are non-governmental. Among the latter, some are indigenous while others are created from outside with or without official assistance. Hence, before we can assess the virtues of 'another development' with its high expectations about LOs and NGOs as triggers of development, we need to know: "What kind of LO and what kind of NGO?" The as yet unanswered question is "Which LOs and NGOs can do what where"?

This anthology by no means attempts to answer all these questions. Much more analysis will be needed before that can be done. But we do hope that the papers presented will contribute to a better understanding of matters involved. The remainder of this chapter adresses two themes. First, considering the extensive confusion of language concerning these matters, we will discuss the use of some central concepts often used in relation to local and non-governmental organizations. Second, we will also present a historical resumé of how organizations and organization-building have been viewed in the development debate during the last decades.

Some conceptual considerations

Central concepts in this anthology are *non-governmental organization (NGO), local organization (LO), participation, empowerment, environment* and *sustainability*. As will be shown below, these concepts are tightly interrelated. In this book they are used in the following manner:

Non-Governmental organization
The emphasis on non-governmental organizations as agents of change in the Third World is a quite recent phenomenon. Nevertheless, in only few years the share of western aid-money channelled through NGOs has multiplied. This is quite strange since little is known about what NGOs are best at -- and under which conditions. Actually, the term NGO does not refer to a certain and well-known type of organization and it seems as if an NGO can be almost anything. As noted by Farrington and Bebbington (1993:3) "everything from a neighbourhood organization concerned with better lighting through to an organization operating globally, such as Oxfam, are equally labelled NGOs".

While demands for "another development" and/or "development from below" is one important (but not the most important -- see section two of this chapter) reason for promotion of NGOs in the Third World, the number of indigenous NGOs to promote appears to be small (*ibid.*). Therefore, western and international NGOs try to establish their own branch organizations as "local" NGOs all over the Third World. Consequently, leadership styles -- and tasks -- differ widely among western-created or supported NGOs. Hence:

> "it is important to distinguish between them according to the nature of their relationship to the rural poor, and their staff composition. On the one hand there are those organizations that are staffed and selected by the people they are meant to serve and represent (such as farmer organizations). ... we call these membership organizations. Non-membership organizations are, by contrast, staffed by people who are socially, professionally and at times ethnically different from their clients. Similarly, the two types of organization have different relationships with the poor who are members of the former, and clients of the latter" (*ibid. p3*).

NGO is thus a blurred concept. It does not refer to size, purpose or type of activity. It is used indiscriminately about western aid-agencies (northern NGOs) and groupings in aid receiving countries (southern NGOs). When governments in the West channel part of their donations through northern NGOs (NONGOs), they still retain some control over its use. Hence, "NONGOs", to the extent that they are not completely independent, should rather be perceived as quasi-NGOs ("QUANGOs"). The same goes for many "SOUNGOs" (southern more or less independent NGOs). Moreover, when aid to the Third World bypasses governments and is allocated to NGOs, governments have implemented cosmetic administrative reforms, turning existing public institutions into "QUANGOs", in order not to loose aid-money. Sometimes, and for the same purpose, they establish their own new and seemingly independent organizations -- "GONGOs" (government organized NGOs) -- or "GINGOs" (government-inspired NGOs) within certain predefined niches. In many cases, therefore, only few so called NGOs are real NGOs.

It has further been noted that some Third World NGOs are run more or less as one man's private business ("PRINGOs" *i.e.* private NGOs). With the recent enormous increase in aid-money channeled through NGOs, it is inevitable that fortune hunters are attracted. Chapter two illustrates how this may affect northern NGOs. Reporting from India, Alström (1994:1) underlines that "tapping some of the foreign aid funds has been an important aim for several newly started still very small but registered societies mushrooming in various parts of the country". Also in other Third World countries it is likely to be the case that "several small NGOs are run almost as a family affair" (*ibid.* p2). However, for anyone to be able to tap aid funds in such a way, he almost certainly has to be well-connected with either local or central government, or both.

But there are other problems involved in defining an NGO. It is often declared that an NGO is -- or should be -- non-profit oriented (Uphoff 1993; Schmale 1993; Farrington & Lewis 1993). This may be a relevant criterion as far as northern NGOs and relief organizations are concerned but it can hardly be an appropriate definition of southern NGOs -- or a prerequisite for being worthy of being included in an analysis of possible change agents for the Third World. If it was, we would be prevented from learning anything from, say, independent rural co-operatives (which do exist).

For a number of reasons it seems meaningless to make any general references to NGOs. But it is not only the unwieldy use of the concept that is disturbing. The term NGO is essentially a negative concept and the only thing that it tells us is that the state is not (openly) involved in an organization's operations and management. If we want to find effective ways to mobilize local people and/or to channel aid-resources to poor groups and under-developed areas, a positive criterion for selecting proper organizations seems warranted and, hence, it might be best to drop the term NGO alltogether.

Local organization
'Local organization', although by no means simple and unambiguous, has the potential of offering such a positive alternative. In recent years 'local organizations' have attracted much attention among social scientists and donor agencies. The concept, however, has many meanings. We therefore find it

necessary to define both its parts, *i.e.* both 'local' and 'organization'. Our criteria of an *organization* are that

(a) it is a more or less formalized grouping of people, joining together to achieve either a shared purpose or, through joint efforts, satisfying individual and shared needs, and

(b) the organization has - or is meant to have - a certain durability.

This definition excludes, for example, 'social movements' which, on the one hand, tend to have a diffuse territorial base and, on the other hand, "are associated with spontaneity, newness, change and instability" (Schmale 1993:6). This also excludes most public service institutions, as well as most commercial firms and private or family business, even if such undertakings must be organized as well. It also excludes traditional 'latent' organizations which can be mobilized for certain labour demanding, recurring but occasional purposes (often mobilized within what Hydén (1983) has called the 'economy of affection') such as roof-laying, well-digging, etc. which are, or have been, common in most rural areas. But as will be clarified below, we do not exclude all types of government organizations.

The second half of the concept -- *local* -- needs some clarification too. In the literature there is, surprisingly, no consensus about what is meant by a local organization. Some see them - even when called 'self-help groups' - as the lowest administrative level ("support groups") in large-scale, top-down delivery systems (see *e.g.* Kirsch *et al* 1980). Schmale (1993:6) defines a 'local' organization as "indigenous, non-governmental and non-profit" oriented. Further, he says, a 'local' organization does not have to be local (*sic!*). It may be "a kind of national umbrella organization for local sub-organizations or divisions". Likewise, many branch offices and/or projects established - and even run - by northern NGOs and operationg at local or regional level in Third World countries are often treated as 'local' organizations.

There is further, in literature, a high degree of confusion concerning local organizations (LOs) and NGOs. This equalization between the two is unfortunate and misleading. In our use of the term, however, 'local' means *local*. Hence, local organizations are to be distinguished from local branches of nationwide parastatals and similar constructs. Rather than constituting a link in a delivery-chain, they represent an attempt to mobilize locally (or regionally) available skills, labour and assets for some productive and/or income-generating purpose. Local organizations, naturally, may have other objectives as well but we believe that, initially at least, satisfaction of perceived basic material needs is a necessary starting point. After all, LOs and NGOs are today propagated as primarily the poors' option to be included in the development process. If and when progress has been made in this field, other objectives can be added. The benefits of the LO's activity may accrue to the members of the group either individually or collectively. Local organizations may evolve spontaneously in response to a perceived need but in many cases an external "catalyst" is likely to be needed. This is also, generally, the basic thought behind 'action research' and 'empowerment' where the role of the outsider is to provoke villagers to find new (joint) solutions to problems they (previously perhaps did not) identify as essential. For an organization to be defined as local, it is essential that responsibility, management and control over strategic decisions are local as well.

This means that certain kinds of government organizations do belong to this category. To the extent that the World Bank's structural adjustment programmes, which for the last decade or so have been implemented (although often reluctantly and to varying degrees) in a great number of Third World countries, do result in administrative deconcentration and devolution of responsibilities to local administrative levels, then, obviously, such "newly liberated" local governments must be considered both as local and as holding a development potential and, hence, to be worthy of investigation. It is of course often the case that administrative reform is merely cosmetic (Cheema & Rondinelli 1983; Holmén 1991) and that it "will just bring 'top-down' micro-development closer to the people" (Fowler 1988:11), However, there is no reason to *à-priori* exclude village councils and local governments from an analysis of what *local* organizations can do. On the contrary, with today's changes in administrative structures, there is even greater reason to include them. But the administrative and institutional framework within which these organizations operate need to be given a considerable attention.

As is the case with NGOs, many types of local organizations -- political, economic, cultural, neighbourhood, etc. -- may be found in the Third World's rural areas. Esman and Uphoff (1988:18) define local organizations as "organizations which act on behalf of and are accountable to their membership and which are involved in development activities (co-operatives, farmers' associations, mothers' clubs, health committees, water users' groups, ethnic unions, tenant leagues, etc.). This distinguishes them from organs of the state and also from more purely social or cultural associations". Local, here, means non-government organizations (NGOs). This is however not how we use the concept. What Esman and Uphoff mean by 'development activities' is less clear. There is, however, in the literature, a widespread inclination to over-emphasize 'progressive values' as a necessary foundation for local organizations if they are to implement development projects successfully (see *e.g.* Mabogunje 1989; Friedmann 1993). Schmale (1993) underlines that local organizations should be non-profit oriented. This is also the view held by, for example, the swedish aid agency (SIDA 1991). Similarly, Farrington and Lewis (1993) in their definition of NGOs exclude both membership service organizations and profit driven organizations. The organizations they choose to focus on - northern based NGOs - often have an outspoken value-driven orientation. To the extent that ideologically based northern aid-NGOs establish or support LOs, this accentuates the risk that (a) external values are imposed on the would-be participants, and (b) that this is done at the expense of business efficiency.

We, on the other hand, do not emphasize some kind of pre-determined values as necessary or sufficient for local organizations to contribute to development. On the contrary, to the extent that values are to play any role in local organization building, it has to be the values of the local constituency. But we do wonder whether it is meaningful to state that local organizations should be non-profit oriented.

In this book we hypothesize that local organizations primarily, but not exclusively, will be constructed to satisfy the economic self-interest of its members. Considering how most Third World rural areas 'lag behind' in development and the extent of rural poverty, it seems appropriate to emphasize satisfaction of basic material needs and the business side of local organizations -- at least to begin with. Although a local organization "may endeavour to satisfy both economic and social aspirations of its members, it seems reasonable to assume that the main reason for a smallholder to join a [local organization] is to realize economic benefits that cannot be obtained on an individual basis" (Gyllström 1991:3). A major investigation of the performance and impact of Third World rural cooperatives (UNRISD 1975:13) found that

> "cooperatives with the least political or social content, being mainly concerned with straightforward economic benefits, may in the end, paradoxically, have a greater impact than those that explicitly but ineffectively seek to transform society".

This, we are quite convinced, goes for most other types of LOs aswell. In spite of many earlier claims to the contrary, Third World peasants (and, of course, other rural inhabitants) are now increasingly recognized as innovative, price-responsive, rational economic decision makers (Gyllström 1991; Holmén 1991; World Bank 1989). As Chambers (1991:87) put it: "small farmers are, after all, professionals. They can not afford not to be". Hence, any effort at rural development and local organization building has to build on the recognition that individual economic self-interest is a decisive cross-cultural force in social reproduction processes (Bates 1981; Gyllström 1991). Economic motives, thus, must be considered as central for people's participation in local organizations. To quote Berthold Brecht: "Erst das Fressen, dann die Moral".

Participation
Participation is increasingly regarded as, perhaps, the most central factor behind success or failure of local organizations. While everybody emphasizes the importance of participation, there is, however, a great deal of confusion as to what the term stands for. For example, "the rhetoric of participation is frequently used by planners to justify - through reference to frequently perfunctory consultation - decisions already taken" (Farrington & Lewis 1993:23). The populist rethoric surrounding the concept participation is, however, being increasingly criticized. In an important paper "Challenging the Populist Perspective", Scoones & Thompson (1993:11) challenge simplistic approaches to agricultural research and extension and point out that: *"... there is no simple 'techno-fix' just as there is no simple 'participation-fix' to the ... problems of the world's resource-poor"*.

Moreover, participation can be spontaneous, induced, coerced, selective, formal, functional, reflective, empowering. In rural parastatals membership and, hence, "participation" has often been coerced (obligatory, state monopolies) or induced (a prerequisite for obtaining subsidized credit, inputs and extension services). In local organizations, on the contrary, spontaneous participation is likely to be the norm, even if potential members can be induced to join the organization for reasons of social pressure, etc. The degree of voluntariness may thus vary even in LOs where membership is officially free. This may affect other types and levels of participation. Even when membership is spontaneous a member may actively seek to make use of only part of the activities pursued by the LO in question. He may, for example, make use of only the economic sides of the activities (buying inputs and selling produce, contributing to and/or using a loan fund) without bothering to vote at elections or accepting to take responsibility as board member, etc. (Holmén 1991). Therefore, also among 'active' participants, it may be useful to make a distinction between *functional* and *reflective* participation. Following Gyllström (1991:18) "Functional participation indicates the degree to which [members] actually take part in their [organizations'] activities as economic actors. By reflective participation is meant the subordination of societal activities to members' conscious reflection and decision-making". Farrington & Lewis use 'functional' in a somewhat different way, saying that participation is functional when farmers are "consulted on the types of technological changes that might meet their needs, and be invited to test and comment on them" (*op. cit.*).

Empowerment
This 'functional participation' they contrast with 'empowerment' which can be considered as both a form of participation and its ultimate objective. In broad terms it "refers to the creation of an environment in which people question and challenge the structural reasons for their poverty through learning and action" (*ibid.*). It is frequently declared that 'empowerment' -- constituting the core of "another development" -- is essentially ideologically motivated (see *e.g.* Friedmann 1993) and it is assumed that empowerment will primarily (if not exclusively) benefit the poor (*ibid.*). This concern for the poor, who are also socially, politically, etc. excluded is of course admirable. But it may also blindfold scholars and substitute speculation and wishful thinking for analysis of existing local realities. As noted by Uphoff (1993:*xiii*), "enthusiasts who are exited by the political and ideological possibilities of NGOs creating an alternative development can become oblivious or apologetic about shortcomings". (See also chapter two). Actually, in the 1990s, about twenty years after the heyday of the dependency paradigm and five years after the collapse of the Sovjet Union, when traditional marxism (if there ever was one) is no longer in vogue, 'empowerment', in many instances, seems to represent class-struggle in disguise. However, it has been questioned whether class-analysis is the most appropriate mode of analysis for large tracts of the Third World and whether classes are the proper foundations for, for example, organization building (see *e.g.* Hydén 1983; Clapham 1985; Hopkins 1988).

Since both top-down and bottom-up programmes are vulnerable to interception by the élite (Chambers 1991), empowerment, often, aims at "strengthening the poors' capacity to demand their rights" (*ibid.*). Hence, "empowerment of the poor is, by definition, a radical undertaking. For precisely this reason, few states can be trusted to promote their interests with vigour" (Simon 1990:19). Local organizations aiming at empowerment may initially be tolerated - sometimes even supported - by central authorities (*e.g.* the Aquino government in the Philippines), but when they grow in importance they are likely to "catch the evil eye of the state".

But there are other risks involved. Often, and possibly as a result of the above reasoning, an exogenous agent acting as 'catalyst' is seen as essential for empowerment to come about and many external NGOs have 'empowerment' as their prime purpose. However, foreign NGOs engaging in 'enabling' and 'empowering' activities in Third World countries actually "may reproduce only new systems of patronage" (Lewis 1993:55) and local groups "may remain dependent upon outsiders' motivation and authority [and] ... the language of conscientization can all too easily turn into rhetoric and be used as a 'buzz-word' by some [external] groups to achieve *their* objectives" (Farrington & Lewis 1993:23; emphasis added). Also Schmale (1993:3) argues that "despite using fashionable jargon such as empowerment, people-centredness and participation, many local organizations continue development work in a top-down, non-participatory and non-sustainable manner". Hence, "the success of [empowerment] has been difficult to evaluate" (Farrington & Lewis *op. cit.*) and, in any case, it is a slow process. The more or less general assumption that NGOs represent a force toward democratic and pluralist civil society has recently begun to be challenged. Fowler (1991) argues that "for Africa the democratizing potential of NGOs is likely to be more limited than is widely held" (quoted from Farrington & Lewis 1993:7).

It has therefore been suggested that it would benefit the poor and vulnerable more if governments (a) improve rural prices and terms of trade and (b) enforce the law (Chambers 1991). Since the poor and powerless are the most vulnerable to corruption and legal abuse, this would benefit them most, eventually enabling them effectively to demand their rights. At the same time, institutional reforms such as administrative deconcentration, price adjustments and law enforcement would, most likely, also provide incentives for local organizations to emerge and/or engage in new and productive projects.

Environment

This leads us to the concept of 'environment' which is not only physical but also legal, economic, social, and organizational. For the purpose of clarity we will comment on these environmental aspects under different headings. However, as the discussion below will emphasize, these various environments are interrelated (but, of course, in different constellations in each specific setting).

As for the *physical environment*, Esman and Uphoff (1988) found that the success of local organizations is often inversely related to supposedly favourable physical environments. They found "a number of environmental conditions generally thought to be undesirable (difficult topography, poor resource endowment, lack of physical infrastructure) to correlate with better local organization performance" (p110).[1] However, they were unable to explain why this is so, merely making a note of this "curious but also encouraging situation to be explored further" (p110).

But the answer need not be so far away. Our argument is that, to a large extent, the physical environment in terms of general agro-ecological conditions will determine *what kind* of organizations we find in different rural areas. In Africa, a high correlation has commonly been found between economic performance and survival rates of state-supported co-operatives and favoured lands (see *e.g.* Gyllström 1991). However, these are certainly not the kind of independent, local self-help organizations upon which so much hope is presently pinned. Rather, they are typical for parastatal organizational structures in government favoured areas. But it seems that it is generally in the less favoured lands that local and non-governmental organizations have been successful, as noted by Esman and Uphoff. It is there that they have increased their presence and found the necessary room for manoeuvre, initiative, etc. (Farrington & Lewis 1993; for concrete examples, see *e.g.* Hopkins *et al.* 1988; Holmén 1989; 1991).

It has been found that, in Asia, the more favoured lands -- the comparatively accessible and populous central and/or irrigated lowland areas -- have for several decades been given priority by public sector institutions. Considering the general scarcity of government resources (financial, administrative, educational, etc.) this is sound economic thinking. In these

---

1 Esman & Uphoff (p.99f) define success as the sum total of the following five variables: economic gains, social benefits, equity effects, reduced discrimination and participation in decision-making.

fairly homogeneous areas governments clearly have an advantage in developing and transferring agricultural technology as farmers' conditions can more easily be replicated on experimental farms and the introduction of new agricultural technology can have wide impact (Farrington & Lewis 1993).

But apart from their in-built potential for fast increases in agricultural productivity, these areas have also caught the attention of Third World governments for a number of political reasons: in many countries they contain the most articulate and politically powerful farmers, and often generate food supplies necessary either for politically important urban electorates or for generating important export earnings.

These priorities in rural development investments towards favoured areas has not only resulted in the presence of parastatals, but also in a strong government influence/control over 'local' organizations. An example of this development is discussed in Jirström's article about Farmers' Organizations in the Muda irrigation scheme in Malaysia (chapter four). Furthermore, farmers in favoured areas also enjoy the advantage of being of interest to the private commercial sector, which can play an important role in providing new agricultural technologies such as seeds, equipment, agro-chemicals and extension services (see the article by Pagaran below (chapter five)).

By contrast, more difficult and/or remote farming areas, less populous and characterized by some combination of low and unreliable rainfall, poor soils, difficult topography and poor infrastructure, have for decades been given low priority by public sector institutions and big-scale commercial companies alike. There are few economies of scale to be gained when clients are widely scattered and, for example, extension services have to be of many specialized kinds with narrow spatial coverage. Moreover, "to the private commercial sector, these [areas] constitute highly fragmented markets, often distant from the main commercial centres and, because of poor infrastructure, difficult and costly to reach" (Farrington & Lewis 1993:5).

Government agencies' lack of success in the remote, diverse and risk-prone areas can, however, not be explained simply by referring to the low priority in resource allocation. The combination of top-down approaches taken by many government agencies and the pursuit of inappropriate research methods explains much of the difficulties in developing and introducing new technologies adapted to the complex and diverse conditions prevailing in the less favoured areas.

In this apparent 'organizational vacuum', the voluntary sector - NGOs - have "moved into 'niches' configured by their skills in certain types of methodology, by the need of their resource-poor 'clients', and the space left by government efforts" (*ibid.* p36). Over the last decade, NGOs have greatly increased their presence in the more difficult areas. It is in these areas that they find the necessary room for manoeuvre or, put it differently, a political space tolerating or even supporting their activities. Information about the physical environment then, forms part of the background knowledge necessary when discussing organizational development in the Third World's rural areas.

As for the *legal environment* of local organizations, the importance of stable institutions (secure property rights, the validity of contracts, and a legal system establishing security in transactions) for development -- and business oriented local organization building -- to come about is now widely acknowledged (see *e.g.* North 1981, 1989; Gunnarsson 1992; Gunnarsson & Holmén 1993). Of fundamental importance here is, of course, the freedom for people to organize. But it is often the case that governments are negative, or even hostile, to organizations they do not control, particularly in the 'high interest areas' mentioned above. In several African countries, for example, unauthorized meetings of more than five (Kenya) or eight (Zambia) people are dispersed by the police as potentially subversive. This makes it unnecessary difficult for boards of directors (not to mention annual meetings) of independent organizations to carry out their tasks properly. We believe, however, that if the business side (as opposed to the political or the 'value' side) of local organizations is emphasized, LOs would be perceived as less of a threat to local elites and central authorities. In this way it can also be assumed that local economic organizations may pave the way for other types of LOs as well. Further aspects of the legal and organizational environment are dealt with in the paper by Hatti and Rundquist (chapter three).

In consonance with the above statements, it is essential for local organizations that the *economic environment* allows them to find their own niches in the market. The structural adjustment programmes presently imposed on several Third World economies has been accused, not only of simplicity, but foremost of sacrificing the poor. And that seems to be a correct assessment, at least in the short run. In the long run, however, it aims, *inter alia*, at widening the market. Important ingredients in this process are elimination of (state) monopolies on agricultural inputs and produce, and price adjustments in favour of agricultural products (World Bank 1989). This is by no means a simple adjustment but it represents a great incentive for rural inhabitants to organize themselves for economic (and other) purposes. In order not to be victimized by stronger, external competitors -- or being left without supplies -

- many categories of rural inhabitants will need to organize to gain economies of scale and/or increase their bargaining power on this emerging market. In this respect, the emerging new economic environment of countries in the South seems to have some important features in common with the economic environment of 19th century Europe and USA. The early European and American cooperatives actually depended on the prevalence of market forces for their success. They were commercial institutions operating in a capitalistic environment. Their aim was not to transform society but rather to improve the economic conditions for their members (Jirström 1989; Holmén 1990).

All rural producers, of course, will not have the same stake in organization building (see chapter two). Looking at the *social environment* of local organizations, it is obvious that in most cases a differentiated social structure is a prerequisite for local organizations to come about. In this connection it must be stressed that nowhere in the contemporary Third World does the rural population consist of one homogeneous group of people with identical needs, interests and resources (if it ever did). Hence, contrary to superimposed, often 'all-inclusive', exogenous organizations, most local (endogenous) organizations are attractive only for certain strata or sub-groups in the local community. In this relation it is common to quote Michels' (1915) declaration that "organization is the weapon of the weak in their struggle with the strong". But it has also been stated that the weak and the poor are so strongly dependent on wealthy patrons that the latter will subjugate the local organization under their interests or even prevent its emergence (*e.g.* Hydén 1983). However, most Third World rural societies can no longer be deemed traditional. At most, they are only semi-traditional. Established social structures and dependencies erode while others evolve. Hence, when the rural economy becomes more diversified and new opportunities open up for the wealthy and well connected, 'traditional' clientelist networks lose in importance (Verhagen 1984; Arn 1988; Holmén 1990, 1991). This, presumably, spreads incentives to organize to different social strata.

Likewise, the risk of fraud and manipulation of funds, etc. by local elites is greater in externally emanating 'local' organizations than in truly local organizations. Esman and Uphoff (1988) underline that the temptation to pocket funds is especially great when money comes from the government or a foreign donor, and is therefore not really local money. This, of course, is not to deny the existence of various "disabilities among the poor that prevent them from taking advantage of the opportunities open to them" (*ibid.* p37). But it should also be underlined that "leadership that arises from within the poor strata does not of itself ensure benefits for them, for social origins are an imperfect predictor of performance on behalf of the disadvantaged" (*ibid.* p253). The problem in this relation is rather, as already underlined, that *it is notoriously difficult to reach the poor* -- *with local organizations or without* (see further chapter two).

Sustainability.
In our use of the concept 'sustainability', we primarily refer to the long-term viability of economically and politically independent LOs in rural development.[2] A prerequisite for an LO to contribute to rural development is that its operations have lasting and positive economic consequences for its members. The emphazis on members' economic self-interest is essential. Any discussion of the economic and political sustainability of organizations must, however, be linked to the questions of a sustainable use of physical resources as well, especially as LOs seem to have their greatest potential in marginal and resource-poor areas.

In the context of organization-led development, two aspects of these questions need to be commented upon here. Firstly, during the last decade the problems of land degradation in many parts of the South has increasingly been connected to the lack of functioning organizations through which local people

---

[2] The need to realize 'sustainable development' has recently been a major theme in most 'development' writings. The Brundtland Report - WCED (1987) - originally defined sustainable development as development "that meets the needs of the present without compromising the ability of future generations to meet their own needs" (p. 43). What a 'need' is is sometimes disputed and there is some disagreement over the meaning of 'sustainable development'. Barbier (1987:103), for example accentuates the needs of the poor and declares that sustainable development means "reducing the absolute poverty of the world's poor through providing lasting and secure livelihoods that minimize resource depletion, environmental degradation, cultural disruption, and social instability". Mayby the major difference concerns whether 'sustainable' refers to physical sustainability or to an extended framework. McCracken and Pretty (1990) found two major schools of interpretation: one meaning 'environmentally sustainable development', *i.e.* "with optimal resource and environmental management over time", and the other meaning sustainable "economic, ecological *and* social development". Obviously, the realization of both these objectives is, in large degree, a matter of organization.

can control and manage the land and water resources in a sustainable way. The role of local organizations for achieving physically and economically viable development is thus receiving a growing attention (see *e.g.* Simon 1990; SIDA 1991; Åkerman 1992).

Secondly, attention is also being drawn to the cases where organizations - typically top-down government controlled service organizations - exist but, due to their inefficiency and non-participatory structures, have a negative impact on the physical environment. Examples of such cases are government planned and administered large-scale irrigation projects in which organizational problems often result in an unsustainable use of the water resources leading to problems of, for example, waterlogging and salinization. Such adversities are sometimes remedied by local, informal organizations *de facto* taking over responsibility from malfunctioning public institutions. Studies from the 'new lands' in the el-Tahrir area in Egypt have, for example, revealed that were it not for the peasants' informal organizations, the irrigation system would not work (Hopkins *et. al.* 1988).

Such experiences are positive indicators. However, as yet they are few and scattered. Therefore, the extent to which -- and the circumstances under which -- local organizations can positively contribute to environmental sustainability need further thorough investigation.

In the above exercise in conceptual clarification we have stressed that a local organization is local. We have also accentuated the business-side of LO-activity, arguing that voluntariness and self-determination are necessary to satisfy the economic self-interests of LO members. We have also underlined that everybody will not benefit (equally) from LOs and that the potential, scope and roles of LOs in contributing to Third World development is highly contextual. In all these statements we seem to differ greatly from most present writers on LOs.

As shown, there is little agreement in the literature on what a local organization is. Likewise, there is little consensus on what the driving force behind the formation of LOs is - or should be ('values', non-profit orientation, 'empowerment', economic self-interest). Neither is there a clear vision of what or how much LOs can achieve in relation to economic development in general -- or for which social groups or strata LOs would be the most relevant instrument. Obviously, the potential of LOs to contribute to development in any sustainable manner depends on a range of environmental (physical, economic, social, etc.) factors. In spite of this conditionality, presently everyone seems to advocate the virtues of LOs as a remedy to Third World poverty. Is this realistic -- and how can this apparent consensus be explained?

Changing Roles for Local Organizations? - A Historical Resumé.

The recent emphasis on the importance of local and non-governmental organizations has been differently explained by different authors. Arn (1988) describes a sequence of evolution of Western development thinking since World War II. In her view, the 1950s were the years when the 'technology gap' was emphasized. The matter was largely seen as a question of transferring the right kinds of technology from the North to the South in order to get development off the ground. When the expected results did not materialize, emphasis was shifted to the 'resource gap' in the 1960s. Underdevelopment "could be overcome by a transfer of resources from the richer to the poorer countries" (p.5). This did not boost development either and by the 1970s attention was turned to the 'organizational gap'. In the 1980s, Arn argues, those advocating organization-building came to be divided into two branches. One 'school' views organization-building as "a necessary, almost technical, instrument in bringing about government policies of rural development, an instrument which implies the involvement of the people concerned" (p.6). The other 'school', which "stresses the need for participation in planning and implementation, has been created during recent years" (*ibid.*). This is probably how many Western promotors of LOs in the Third World wish to see things. However, as will be shown below, this supposedly linear evolution of 'development understanding' is highly simplified and partly misgiving. Moreover, it may be more self-legitimating than concerned with the perceived needs of would-be beneficiaries. As Arn points out, the latter 'school' of thought -- often with an outspoken emphasis on 'empowerment' and 'participatory fixes' -- represents *"an ideological orientation which is becoming increasingly strong in the developed countries, but which may be less important today among the poor in the Third World"* (*ibid;* emphasis added).

Also Schmale (1993) directs attention to the self-interests of those engaged in the aid business. Both development aid in general and Third World governments in particular have been severely criticized in recent years. On the one hand, "the renewed focus on the NGO sector [may therefore be] a result of pressures in Northern countries to find more effective ways of spending aid money" (Schmale 1993:1). To make aid more effective would, of course, be a legitimate objective. However, Schmale is more dubious about the real motive behind this recent re-orientation of organizational support. He finds that "the aid business has become self-supporting; it permanently looks for new tasks to ensure its continued existence" (p.25; a good illustration is given in chapter two). In these days when "government bashing" (Hettne 1992:17) has become so fashionable, efforts to circumvent the state and strengthen NGOs may be the obvious means for aid agencies to remain in business - despite Arn's notion that this approach may be less relevant to satisfy locally perceived needs.

That any organization's staff has a self-interest in preserving the organization, and that the staff's guiding ideology may change in order to preserve this self-interest, is a familiar story among those acquainted with organization theory. However, to view all leading aid-agency representatives as opportunists would be an exaggeration. Many of those working in aid agencies *are* sincerely concerned about poverty and underdevelopment in the countries of the South. There is also among many theorists as well as practitioners a firm belief that development *must* come from 'below' -- that development must be accomplished by the people, not organized for them.

Likewise, Arn's 'evolutionary scheme' is somewhat misgiving. Development theorists and aid agencies did not suddenly stumble on the 'matter of organization' in the 1970s. On the contrary, a number of efforts at organization-building -- voluntary co-operatives, community development schemes, state-supervised co-operatives, farmers' associations, non-governmental organizations -- have been tried in large parts of the Third World since the 1950s. In all these different kinds of organizations self-help on a co-operative basis as well as the founding of activities on the villagers' perceived needs were -- theoretically at least -- accentuated (see *e.g.* Holdcroft 1982). There is nothing new about that. What is new, however, is a growing awareness that 'development' is a complex matter and that we are not likely to find any standard recipes for its realization. As geographers have been keen to point out, 'development', inevitably, is the result of a combination of grand processes and local realities (Aase 1990; Brown 1989). In this relation, the emergence of a multitude of LOs would lead to greater variability and, possibly, to better local resource utilization in the South.

During the last half of the twentieth century, the development of the poor countries in Asia, Africa and Latin America has been the concern of many organizations and individuals in both the First and the Third Worlds. During the period of fast economic growth in the West that accompanied the rebuilding of Europe and Japan in the early post-war period, there was widespread optimism about man's ability to realize planned, progressive change and it was relatively easy to mobilize support for development aid. 'Development' was often seen as rather unproblematic. Comparatively simple solutions to under-development were presented and the West was generally regarded as an example for others to follow. This, it was argued, poor countries could do by introducing the same 'rationality' and the same type of organizations that had made the West rich. There was no great need to legitimate donor agencies' activities and private, national and international aid-agencies mushroomed in the rich countries.

However, with the exception of the East Asian NICs, the Third World did not develop -- at least not in the way it was expected.[3] Actually, in many places the situation grew worse. Parallel to the spreading awareness that 'development' is a much more complicated process than previously assumed, it

---

3 A perhaps disturbing fact is that in the few countries that are today commonly referred to as - virtually the only - 'late developers' or 'miracle economies' (Taiwan and South Korea), LOs and NGOs have not been prominent and 'empowerment' as a precondition for development has been completely out of question. As Moore (1988:132), writing about these two countries, reveals: "Local Farmers' Associations and Irrigation Associations maintain, despite their formal non-governmental status, 'security' departments staffed by central Party or security personnel but financed by the Associations themselves. The utility of the Farmers' and Irrigation Associations as strategic institutions from which to maintain political surveillance at local level was enhanced by the policy towards 'private' associations pursued ... in agriculture as in all spheres of public activity. Only officially recognised and registered associations may function. Those which are recognized - and closely controlled politically - are given *de facto* monopolies. Where organizations do not exist, they are created on state initiative as a preemptive measure. The only farmers' organisations officially tolerated are the Farmers' and Irrigation Associations and the marketing 'cooperatives' mentioned above".

was also shown that the West had not followed one development path but several (see *e.g.* Senghaas 1985). To regard the West as one example for others to follow, therefore, is an illusion. Also, it was increasingly realized that rationality is contextual and organizational behaviour changes with time and place.

Furthermore, when the economic growth in the West began to slow down as the rebuilding process after the Second World War seemed to be 'completed', development aid came to be seen as costly and was increasingly questioned. It was pointed out that 'aid' was highly politicized and ineffective. Primarily, established forms of aid giving were criticized for leading to 'aid-dependency' and for not reaching those most in need. Increasingly, the 'soft' and 'overdeveloped' Third World state - through which most development-aid had been channelled - came to be seen as one of the greatest obstacles to Third World development.

This led to several reactions, for example, the IMF's and the World Bank's demands for 'structural adjustment' as a condition for continued western aid. Parallel to this were claims that development had to come from 'below' and that it must be based on the principle of self-help. Local organizations were to substitute for large-scale and centralized development schemes and parastatal organizations with nation-wide coverage. The many calls for de-officialization of Third World co-operative organizations is a case in point (*e.g.* UNRISD 1975; Hanel 1985; Holmén 1990; Gyllström 1991). In line with this it has increasingly been argued that the state should be by-passed as development agent and instead NGOs have been presented as the 'key' to successful implementation of aid programmes in poor countries (WCED 1987; WDR 1992).

This, however, appears as yet another set of simplifications and the same belief in simple solutions that has previously failed. The Third World is as diverse as the rest of the world and "to generalize about the state and rural development in the South is rash. Almost any statement needs qualification" (Chambers 1989:1). Nevertheless, irrespective of varying local preconditions, and neglecting that "government stewardship... has shown a mixed record of successes and failure" (WDR 1992:144), "the IMF tends to treat all countries in the same manner, and to demand the same sort of market-oriented economic reforms everywhere" (Louvet 1989:18).

It may be perfectly rational from a theoretical neo-classical economic point of view to declare that 'less government is always better government'. The problem with neo-classical economy, however, is that it "simply assumes away all the relevant issues" (North 1989). Contemporary advocates of 'less government' tend to overlook that "the argument for statism was normally not that state-organized economic activities were inherently superior, but that they were a substitute for a defective market. Now instead, a defective market is seen as a substitute for a defective state" (Hettne 1992:5).

Economic development does not come about in simplified models. It has to take its point of departure in existing geographical, demographical, cultural, historical, and institutional realities. These differ from place to place and from region to region and they further change over time. Therefore, in the above reasoning, the obvious lesson to be learned from past experience -- that there are no standard solutions to development -- has not been given the attention it deserves. Instead major development organizations have found new standard solutions to propagate. One may wonder whether this is rational.

The apparent contemporary western consensus about the virtues of LOs and NGOs is, however, rather hollow and not at all standardized. As Gutto (1993:142) points out, promotors of NGOs have widely diverging views on their roles and tasks. Some expect them to contribute to the 'rolling back' of the Third World state and to create "new forms of state or non-state arrangements which are more stable *but which are still subordinate and controlled from outside*". The externally supported 'contras' in Nicaragua is one case in point, the 'misuse' of NGOs to undermine the government in and recolonize Mocambique is another (see e.g. Hanlon 1991). Others want NGOs to "contain and 'organize' the people" so as to "prevent radical revolutionary change or anarchy" (Gutto *op. cit.*). Therefore, many local NGOs are "started by well-educated, charismatic rich men, who seriously want to combat poverty (and political unrest)" (Runnquist 1993:37). Still others maintain that NGOs represent "revolutionary potentials which may be nurtured to build alternative forms of democracy" (Gutto *op. cit.*; see also Simon 1990; Friedmann 1993).

Also, when discussing NGOs in connection with liberalization, self-help and 'development from below', it is often implicit that we talk about Third World NGOs. However, it seems that in practice it is western NGOs we are dealing with. Many western NGOs are used as channels for government money which in some cases makes up a major part of their budgets. For example, the proportion of Swedish bilateral aid channelled through Swedish NGO's increased from 5 % in 1980/81 to 11% in 1991/92 (SOU 1993) and to 25 % in 1992/93 (SIDA 1993). On a global scale, international funds channelled through NGOs doubled from US$ 3,6 billion in 1983 to US$ 7 billion in 1990 - the equivalent of 16 % of total bilateral aid flows in that year

(Farrington & Lewis 1993). Considering that money thus allocated is not given without strings attached it would, in many cases, be preferable to speak of northern NGOs as quasi-NGOs.

Moreover, in the rich world there are many types of non-governmental organizations involved in the 'aid-business'.[4] To assemble them all under one rubric - NGOs - is not very clarifying. Under this label can be found a wide range of organizations with various altruistic, as well as political, religious or otherwise ideological underpinnings. It is therefore no guarantee that aid through NGOs will be less biased than official aid. This may reduce these organizations' efficiency as development agents.

The sudden growth in sheer numbers of NGOs may be another cause of inefficency. If the previous situation, with national donor agencies - each with "its own particular sectoral preferences and set of procedures" (Simon & Rakodi 1990:255) - lead to administrative overload and lack of coordination within the state's planning organs, the new approach can actually make things worse. While, in the 1980s, it was noted that, for example, "Zambia has as many agricultural policies as foreign donors" (*ibid.* p256), it is now reported that "In some developing countries there are already more than a 1000 private international NGOs stepping on each other's toes and fighting for the few good opportunities to spend aid effectively" (Musto 1987; quoted from Schmale 1993:32). But even if numbers of NGOs and LOs -- and of rural policies -- are great, their contributions to development may be rather limited. In India, for example, "within certain districts ... NGOs ... overlap and compete for clients, while in other areas there are hardly any NGOs active on the ground" (Robinson *et al.* 199x:93). Uphoff (1993:*xiv*) found himself forced to admit that "the potential for disappointment and even disaster with NGOs looms large".

Furthermore, the enthusiasm - often ideologically motivated - which is said to be a strength of many (Western) NGOs, may be a disadvantage. To the extent that this enthusiasm stems from the belief that the NGO staff is 'doing good', it may prevent critical evaluation of the appropriateness and effects of projects undertaken. Riddell (1990:7f), in an investigation of British NGOs, found that "NGO projects and programmes are rarely undertaken with the benefits of a pre-feasibility study, any sort of base-line study or any monitoring of a control group". He also found that

---

4 Louvet (1989:71) estimates that there are about 2200 NGOs in the industrialized countries and between 10 000 and 20 000 on the receiving side in the Third World countries.

> "The vast majority of projects and programmes funded by ... NGOs in developing countries are not subject to any sort of formal evaluation, and they are not bound to specified cycles of expenditure for committed support, as is common in official aid projects. The majority of NGOs do not carry out *any* evaluations beyond normal office procedures of project report-back and financial audit (not all ... NGOs have formalised even these procedures for all of their interventions in developing countries).

In the past, many NGOs have been engaged in relief work rather than in development assistance. In some cases it appears as essential for NGOs that this role is perpetuated. It is well known that a large part of aid resources channelled through official institutions is consumed within the organizations themselves and that only a small part reaches the target groups. On the contrary, in many NGOs only a minor part tends to be used up by aid administration and most resources reach the target groups. However, while it is a general policy in bilateral aid agencies that their personnel make themselves dispensable and official projects always have a (relatively short) terminating date, many NGOs find it very difficult to withdraw from initiated projects. For many of those engaged in NGOs it is an end in itself to remain in business -- not to end it. In many cases, 'being there' appears to be the prime objective. This may explain why, in many cases, NGOs seek visibility and "attack symptoms, not causes" (Chambers 1991:164).

Nevertheless, it is commonly asserted that NGOs "seem to be comparatively effective" (see *e.g.* Andersson *et. al.* 1984). One often mentioned advantage is that they sometimes "can reach such target groups that government organizations wish to support but can not reach directly" (Louvet 1989:71). There is little doubt that NGOs can have a significant role to play in micro-development in various parts of the Third World. They are more flexible and often show greater responsiveness to local needs and preconditions than large-scale, expert-led organizations and authorities. One aspect of this view is that many NGOs are concerned with technologies that are more environmentally sustainable than those relying on high inputs of agrochemicals and mechanical power. It is generally expected that these organizations, which typically possess location-specific knowledge about agro-ecological conditions, will contribute to a sustainable use of land and water resources. This assumed capacity has contributed to the growing interest among aid agencies to channel funds to the developing countries through NGOs.

However, one should not exaggerate the expectations about how much NGOs and LOs can accomplish. In most cases, both the projects and the results of NGOs are limited (*ibid.*). As Upphoff (1993:*xiv*) reveals:

> "A highly respected NGO leader in India when I asked him how many NGOs in his country were both 'genuine' and effective, sadly guessed this would be around 20 percent. Both of us regretted that proponents of the NGO alternative were not more critical of the limitations and even deceptions one could find on close examination of this heterogeneous category of organizations".

Voluntary organizations are often ineffective and hampered by limited funds, lack of knowledge and contacts, etc. But they manage to do something and they do

> "have an advantage in their small-scale, in their flexibility, their limited bureaucracy and direct control over field activities. Contrary to governmental aid organizations, they often operate in an atmosphere of enthusiasm. On the other hand, these advantages are also their most serious limitations. Voluntary organizations must not grow too big ... lest their activities will be hampered by the same problems affecting bilateral development co-operation" (Andersson *et. al.* 1984:220).

Hence, also LO and NGO activities may lead to aid dependency. For such reasons it has been found that the comparative advantages of NGOs are often only potential -- seldom exploited -- advantages and that far-reaching organizational changes have to be made when decisions are taken to move from relief to development (Fowler 1988).

Concluding Remark

There has, for a long time, been a marked tendency in the 'development' debate to present one or another standard recommendation for the achievement of growth, progress or whatever. This, obviously is a misconception -- there are no panacea for development. Moreover, it seems that old recipes are sometimes presented under new labels to -- semantically at least -- comply with the latest development fashion. In the case of local organizations as instruments for development this is quite clear. While their external promoters remain more or less the same type of organizations (embracing the same vested interests), support to LOs has been differently motivated. First they were to be local self-help organizations, then junior partners to the state or 'delivery organizations'. Now they are presented as alternatives to the state.

However, regardless of the perception of the role of LOs, there are, and will always be, clear limitations as to what they can accomplish. It is probably a correct assessment that without local organizations the prospects for development look gloomy indeed. However, they can not do it all. In many cases a healthy independence from the state will be a prerequisite for the success of LOs. In other cases, however, some kind of symbiosis with the state will be necessary. The state cannot simply be wished away. Although there is a plentiful of examples of corrupt, 'cleptocratic' and otherwise "irrational" governments in the Third World -- without the state's support the lot of the poor can not be significantly improved and the creation of effective LOs, in most cases, requires a strong state.

A strong state, however, is not the same as a large and 'overdeveloped' state involved in a maximum of transactions. The proper relation between state and 'civil society' will in each case be determined by local realities, historical circumstances and the 'level' of development attained. But, whatever the specific situation, in the complex orchestration of 'development' each actor has to do what he is good at and abstain from tampering with matters others could perform better. It is for the state to supply public goods and to establish the institutions necessary for local organizations to perform their tasks. This means extending - and in some cases even creating - an organizational space where local organizations can find the necessary manoevering room to respond to local needs.

References

Aase TH (1990): 'En geografi-flykting krysser sitt spor - i Pakistan.' In (Eds.) Hesselberg A Barkved: *Utviklingsgeografi*. Geografi i Bergen, No. 143, Department of Geography, University of Bergen.

Alström S (1994): *Thoughts on Non-Governmental organizations for Rural Change in India*. Unpublished seminar paper, Department of Social and Economic Geography, University of Lund.

Andersson C, Heikensten L, de Vylder S (1984): *Bistånd i kris - en bok om svensk u-landspolitik.* Stockholm, Liber.

Arn A-L (1988): *The Making of Institutions and Leaders at Rice Root Level: Inside the Rural Works Programme in Southern Bangladesh.* CDR Project Paper 88,3. Copenhagen, Centre for Development Research.

Barbier EB (1987): 'The Concept of sustainable Economic Development'. *Environmental Conservation, 14 (2), pp101-110.*

Bates R (1981): *Markets and States in Tropical Africa: The Political Basis of Agricultural Policies.* Berkley, University of California Press.

Brown LA (1989): 'Reflections on Third World Development: Ground Level Reality, Exogenous Forces, and Conventional Paradigms.' *Economic Geography.* Vol. 64, pp 255-278.

Chambers R (1988): 'Bureaucratic Reversals and Local Diversity'. *IDS-Bulletin* No. 19, Vol. 4, pp50-56.

Chambers R (1989): *The State and Rural Development: Ideologies and an Agenda for the 1990s.* IDS-Discussion Paper, No. 269. Institute of Development Studies, Sussex.

Chambers R (1991): *Rural Development - Putting the Last First.* London, Longman.

Cheema GS, Rondinelli DA (1983): *Decentralization and Development.* Beverly Hills, UNCRD, Sage Publ.

Clapham C (1985): *Third World Politics - An Introduction.* London, Croom Helm.

Esman MJ, Uphoff NT (1988): *Local Organizations - Intermediaries in Rural Development.* Cornell University Press, Ithaca and London.

Farrington J, Bebbington A (1993): *Reluctant Partners? NGOs, the State and Sustainable Agricultural Development.* Routledge, London.

Farrington J, Lewis DJ (1993): *Non-Governmental Organizations and the State in Asia.* London & New York, Routledge.

Fowler A (1988): *Non-governmental Organizations in Africa: Achieving Comparative Advantage in Relief and Micro-development.* IDS, Discussion Paper No. 249.

Friedmann J (1993): *Empowerment - The Politics of Alternative Development.* Blackwell, Oxford.

Gunnarsson C (1992): 'Staten och institutionerna'. In (Ed.) Söderström: *Den offentliga sektorn.* SNS Förlag, Stockholm, pp26-87.

Gunnarsson C, Holmén H (1993): *'Development, Development Models and Institutions Research'.* Paper presented at the VIIth General EADI-Conference, Berlin 15-18 sept. 1993.

Gunnarsson C, Holmén H (1994): 'Is there an East Asian Model?' in (Ed) Lauritzson G: *Cooperation East and West - Continued. Ten Years with the Programme for East and Southeast Asian Studies.* Lund University, Studentlitteratur, Lund.

Gutto S (1993): *Human and Peoples' Rights for the Opressed.* Lund Studies in Law and Society 3. Lund University Press.

Gyllström B (1991): *State Administered Rural Change - Agricultural Co-operatives in Kenya.* London and New York, Routledge.

Hanel A (1985): 'Instruments of Self-Help Promotion - an Introduction to the Subject Matter. In: *Promotion of Self-Help Organizations.* Sankt Augustin, Konrad Adenauer-Stiftung, pp179-199.

Hanlon J (1991): *Mozambique - Who Calls the Shots?* London, James Curry.

Hesselberg J (1985): 'Retninger i utviklingsgeografi'. *Nordisk Samhällsgeografisk Tidskrift.* No. 2, pp18-27.

Hettne B (1992): *The Future of Development Studies.* Paper presented at the 40th Anniversary of ISS. Oct. 1992.

Holdcroft LE (1982): 'The Rise and Fall of Community Development in Developing Countries, 1950-1965: A Critical Analysis and Implications'. in (Eds.) Jones & Rolls: *Progress in Rural Extension and Community Development.* John Wiley and Sons Ltd. pp207-231.

Holmén H (1989): 'Basaisa, en by i Nildeltat - 8 år senare.' *Geografiska Notiser,* No. 1, pp22-30.

Holmén H (1990): *State, Co-operatives and Development in Africa.* Uppsala, The Scandinavian Institute of African Studies, Research Report No. 86.

Holmén H (1991): *Building Organizations for Rural Development: State and Cooperatives in Egypt.* Lund, Lund University Press.

Hopkins N (1988): *Agrarian Transformation in Egypt.* Cairo, The American University in Cairo Press.

Hopkins N, el-Haydary A, el-Zoghby S, Saad R & Bahaa el-Din ZA (1988): 'Participation and Community in the Egyptian new Lands: the Case of South Tahrir'. *Cairo Papers in Social Science,* Vol 11, Mon 1, Spring 1988. The American University in Cairo Press.

Hydén G (1983): *No Shortcuts to Progress - African development management in perspective.* London & New Dehli, Heinemann.

Jirström M (1989): *Agricultural Cooperatives in Zimbabwe.* Department of Social and economic Geography, Lund University, Rapporter och Notiser No. 90

Kirsch O, Benjacov A, Schujmann L (1980): *The Role of Self-Help Groups in Rural Development Projects.* Breitenbach Publ., Saarbrücken and Fort Lauderdale.

Lewis DJ (1993): 'Overview: NGO-Government Interaction in Bangladesh.' In (Eds): Farrington & Lewis: *Non-Governmental Organizations and the State in Asia.* Routledge, London & New York, pp47-58.

Louvet DK (1989): *Realpolitik og Udviklingsbistand. En introduktion til international bistandspolitik.* Skive, Mellemfolkeligt Samvirke.

Lund R (1986): 'Development Geography, Development Orientation and Planning Focus'. In (Ed) Jones: *Welfare and Environment.* Tapir, Oslo, pp121-142.

Mabogunje A (1989): *The Development Process: A Spatial Perspective.* London, Unwin Hyman.

McCracken JA, Pretty JN (1990): *Glossary of Selected Terms in Sustainable Agriculture.* IIED, London.

North D (1981): *Structure and Change in Economic History.* WW Northon & Co.

North D (1989): 'Institutions and Economic Growth: An Historical Introduction'. *World Development.* Vol. 17, No. 9, pp1319-1332.

Prakash D (1992): *Sustaining Environment Through Cooperative Action.* New Delhi, ICA.

Riddell R (1990): *Evaluating NGO Approaches to Alleviating Poverty in Developing Countries.* ODI Working Paper No. 37. Overseas Development Institute, London.

Robinson M, Farrington J, Satish S (1993): 'Overview: NGO-Government Interaction in India.'. in (Eds) Farrington & Lewis: *NGOs and the State in Asia.* London & New York, Routledge. pp91-101.

Runnquist J (1993): 'Bangladesh - Country, programme and project review.' *IRDCurrents,* No. 6, Oct. pp 36f.

Schmale M (1993): *The Role of Local Organizations in Third World Development.* Avebury, Aldershot.

Scoones I, Thompson J (1993): *Challenging the Populist Perspective: Rural People's Knowledge, Agricultural Research and Extension Practice.* Discussion Paper 332, December, Institute of Development Studies.

Senghaas D (1985): *The European Experience - a Historical Critique of Development Theory.* Leamington Spa/Dover, Berg Publ.

SIDA - Swedish International Development Authority -(1991): *Miljö och fattigdom: Handlingslinjer för SIDAs bistånd.* Stockholm.

SIDA - Swedish International Development Authority - (1993): *Bistånd, mål och resultat. SIDAs verksamhet budgetåret 1992/93.* Norrtälje.

Simon D (ed.) (1990): *Third World Regional Development.* London, Paul Chapman Publ. Ltd.

Simon D, Rakodi C (1990): 'Conclusions and Prospects: What Future for Regional Planning?' In (Ed) Simon: *Third World Regional Development.* London, Paul Chapman Publ. pp249-260.

SOU 1993:1. *Styrnings- och samarbetsformer i biståndet.* Stockholm, Nordstedts.

UNRISD (1975): *Rural Co-operatives as Agents of Change: a Research Report and a Debate.* Geneva, UNRISD.

Uphoff N (1993): 'Foreword' to (Eds) Farrington & Bebbington: *Reluctant Partners? NGOs, the State and Sustainable Agricultural Development.* Routledge, London.

Verhagen K (1984): *Cooperation for Survival.* Royal Tropical Institute, Amsterdam/ICA, Doordrecht.

WDR *(World Development Report)* 1992.

World Bank (1989): *Sub-Saharan Africa: From Crisis to Sustainable Growth.* Washington DC, The World Bank.

World Commission on Environment and Development (1987): *Our Common Future.* Oxford University Press, Oxford.

Åkerman J (1992): 'Aspects on peoples' participation in soil and water conservation issues - an institutional approach.' In Jirström & Rundquist (Eds.): *Physical, Social and Economic Aspects of Environmental Degradation.* Rapporter och Notiser Nr 108. Department for Social and Economic Geography, Lund University. pp79-85.

Chapter Two

CO-OPERATIVES AND THE ENVIRONMENTAL CHALLENGE

- What Can Local Organizations Do?

By Hans Holmén

Introduction

This paper discusses expectations and proclamations about what co-operatives may achieve as development instruments in general and as means for environmental protection in particular. It then compares these expectations with empirical observations about what has actually been achieved. Special emphasis is given to three inter-related topics, namely: poverty alleviation, women's emancipation and soil conservation. It is shown that expectations are often unrealistic and ill-founded. Although the focus in this paper is on co-operatives, experiences from other local NGOs are included. It will be shown that the co-operative experience does not differ much from other local and non-governmental organizations aiming to promote development in the Third World. It is concluded that if NGOs are to make a positive contribution to Third World development, a more realistic appreciation of what these types of organizations can achieve would save much time and effort and cause less frustration - not least at the local level.

Co-operative organizations are particularly relevant for an investigation as outlined above. First, because they are based on a participatory concept: local people joining together to achieve a common goal through an organization characterized by democratic control and equitable contributions and risk sharing. A second reason is that co-operatives are well-established in most countries in the Third World. Their apex-organization, the International Cooperative Alliance (ICA) is not only one of the oldest international NGOs in the world. Founded in London in 1895, the ICA now claims to reach "over 648 million individual members in ... 77 countries" (Prakash 1992). Thirdly, in a great number of Third World countries state influence over co-operative affairs is now giving way for voluntariness, self-determination and market orientation of activities. Co-operatives, thus, are in many cases transformed from parastatals to more genuine local organizations. Hence, an investigation of recent experiences of co-operatives and rural development promotion may enhance our knowledge about what realistically can be expected from development oriented NGOs.

The Environmental Challenge

As the 20th century comes to a close, the rich part of the world can look back upon 150 to 200 years of unprecedented growth and 'development'. For the great number of poor countries on earth, this period has not meant the same betterment of life situations and living standards. But it has led to a previously unimaginable growth in populations. Although the rate of population growth has declined in most parts of the Third World, the world population has never grown as fast as presently if measured in real numbers. As development to a great extent has been blocked or retarded in the poor countries, their growing populations are forced to tax the natural environment that forms the basis for their lifes and economies. With little else than primary production to fall back upon, this has resulted in alarming rates of erosion, soil degradation, deforestation, etc. Egypt, for example, looses annually about one half percent of its agricultural land due to unsuitable irrigation and land management techniques and another half percent due to urban and village sprawl (Holmén 1991). On a global scale, it has been estimated that the total 'loss of land to development' amounts to 2,6 million hectars per year (Pierce 1990) - a figure equalling the total cultivated area of Denmark.

But also in the 'developed' countries production techniques and consumption patterns are causing great damage in the form of waste mountains and pollution of air, soil and water. In fact, these problems are so great that they are seen to threaten man's future existence on earth. In spite of repeated calls for sustainable development and ecological consciousness (The Stockholm Conference 1972, IUCNs World Conservation Programme 1980, the

Brundtland Report 1988), this awareness has been slow to come about. Finally, in the early 1990s a sudden global mobilization of environmentally good forces has been called upon, most visibly manifested in the Rio Conference in 1992 and the proclamation of the 5th of May 1992 as the "World Environment Day".

Presumptuous Declarations and Unrealistic Expectations

Co-operatives all over the world, and primarily their apex organization ICA (the International Co-operative Alliance), have been quick to respond to this appeal. The matter *is* serious and naturally it is pleasing to find that co-operators regard themselves and their organizations as being part of the 'good' forces now endeavouring to overcome the environmental challenge. It is therefore encouraging to see that the co-operative movement considers itself "to be aware of the environmental problems ... and committed to working towards their resolution" (ICA 1990a:79). It is also a good sign that the various regional ICA organs have been producing and distributing 'awareness raising' booklets on environmental matters and spreading tips about what can be done locally to protect the environment (*e.g.* "A Place to Live" 1990 and "Environment and Co-operatives" 1992).

However, one does wonder about certain assertions concerning the capacity of co-operatives in relation to environmental protection. It has, for example, been declared that co-operatives are "*ideally placed* to implement activities dealing with the protection of the environment as well as with sustainable development" (ICA 1992b:1). As if that was not enough, it has also been stated that in relation to environmentally sound development "co-operatives in many parts of the world have shown the way" (Prakash 1990:*i*) and that "co-operatives are the *best and most appropriate institutions to ... save the earth*" (*ibid*:22). Hence, co-operatives are "expected to play a *leading role* in sustainable development activities *in any country or region*" (ICA 1992a:222, emphasis added).

Are such declarations realistic assessments of the role co-operatives can play in environmental protection, or are they just another effort to boost the co-operative idea as such? Otherwise expressed, is the concern primarily about the future of co-operatives or is it about the future of the environment? The question is relevant because it *is* disturbing to find a recent book on

39

"Environment and Co-operatives" (ICA 1992c:7) mentioning that, after all, "the environmental programme gives a favourable image of the whole co-operative sector" (Kemppinen 1992:10).

A number of questions demand answers in relation to the above statements. First, on what grounds can it be asserted that co-operatives are "ideally placed" superior institutions which can assume a "leading role" in environmental protection? Second, in what parts of the world would that be the case, in the rich or in the poor countries? Third, are these assertions a reflection of faith or merely a symptom of opportunism in co-operative marketing?

As far as faith is concerned, having dealt with co-operators in a number of countries for the last ten years, it is astonishing how much devotion to co-operation one finds within various cooperative movements. When confronted with the tremendous development tasks facing most Third World co-operatives, it is not uncommon to hear co-operators declare that "you must believe in what you are doing". And that is of course correct, provided that 'believe' is not understood in a religious sense. However, many western co-operators, not least in aid sections, seem to be permeated by a kind of 'missionary spirit'. Co-operatives appear as a sacred form of organization with an alleged capability to solve almost all mankind's problems. All that is needed is to embrace the co-operative 'ethos' and believe in co-operation.

This preoccupation with belief has been illustrated by a reluctance to critically evaluate co-operative impact and performance among many of those belonging to the 'movement'. For example, in 1975, a major investigation of the *practice* and effects of Third World co-operatives was presented (UNRISD 1975). It stated that, due to subordination under governments and the frequent use of co-operatives for political and non-economic purposes, Third World co-operatives seldom realized the development goals set for them. The report was not allowed to be published without a section including a 'debate' about its findings. In this debate members of the 'movement' and representatives of co-operative aid agencies aired their discontent with the conclusions as if it was the *'ethos'* and *principles* of co-operation which were being questioned, which was not the case (see also Apthorpe & Gasper 1982).

Among representatives of the 'international co-operative movement' it is widely held that co-operation is not only a business organization but, primarily, "a way of life" (Hasselmann 1971) and "the only form of enterprise that represents an ideology" (Johansson 1980). The implicit message is that if you are a cooperator then you are one of the good guys and if only the cooperative ideas were more widely adopted, the world would be a better one. If only the basic cooperative values, identified by Marcus (1988:21) as "devotion, democracy, honesty and care", were allowed to influence mankind more, development would not be so problematic. But is it really that simple?

This uncritical faith in the capacity of the sacred organization has lead to a number of similarly bold statements over the years. It has been declared that co-operatives can "solve the problem of food supply in the Third World" (Bonow 1969), that they can improve the situation of the poor (COPAC 1978; Young *et. al.* 1981), extend democracy (Klöwer 1977), and improve the situation of women (Rupena-Osolnik 1978). But that is not all. Co-operatives are said to represent "the most valid of the solutions for the Third World and its problems" (Konopnicki 1978) and it is believed that "in the long run" co-operatives will "resolve most if not all problems of development" (ICA 1978), and even solve the 'population problem' (Mabogunje 1982). And now the turn has come to environmental protection...

It must be wonderful to believe so strongly in what one is doing and to have such faith in the capability of one type of organization to solve so many and so difficult problems of (under)development. That is, if it is faith that causes representatives of the cooperative movement to make these bold statements? Maybe it is instead *lack of faith* that lies behind such declarations? After all, the latest two decades have witnessed what is commonly known as a global 'cooperative crisis', caused by conflict of interest and a wide gap between members' and official representatives' aspirations (see *e.g.* Dülfer 1975; Karlander 1981; Markus 1988).

In order to mobilize support and devotion among members and functionaries and in order to shake off the sense of crisis, co-operators often seem tempted to 'jump on the band wagon' as soon as mass media and/or organizations like the UN emphasize new problems needing to be solved. Since a large part of NGO aid is financed over national budgets, it is of vital importance for intermediaries to rapidly incorporate such signals in their strategies. There is nothing strange about that.

However, such adaptability not only has implications for the roles NGOs are expected to play in relation to development in general and environmental protection in particular. It also has implications for the 'ethos' permeating many NGOs. In the case of co-operatives, they were originally established as voluntary and democratically controlled self-help organizations. People with limited means pooled resources to gain greater bargaining power and/or to invest for a common purpose. As the 'movement' spread over earth, more and more co-operative organizations, especially in the Third World, were established and controlled by governments, often in conjunction with foreign promotors of co-operation. Membership was either compulsory or a precondition for subsidized credit. In that way the co-operative ethos was compromized but that apparently did not bother the apex organization ICA very much. The ICA has been quite content counting numbers of 'affiliated' members and national 'co-operative' organizations. Since the ICA Congress formulating the co-operative principles did not manage to solve the question about the relation between co-operatives and the state, it has become increasingly obscure what a co-operative actually is (Holmén 1990). Too many engaged co-operators have abstained from clarifying what it is they want to support - local co-opera*tion* i.e. people joining together for a shared purpose, or formally registered 'co-opera*tives*' i.e. organizations given an official label but with little room for local initiative and influence.

Until the late 1980s a mass of co-operative literature continued to emphasize the need of government support for co-operative success and that co-operatives should operate 'hand in hand' with governments. During the 1980s, however, this view of co-operatives was increasingly questioned and critics of existing co-operative structures advocated a liberation of co-operatives and for the need to turn them into self-help organizations rather than appendices to the central government (see, for example, Gyllström 1991; Holmén 1990, 1991; Holmén & Öjermark 1992). This was also the time when the World Bank's and the IMF's demands for 'structural adjustment' gained momentum. In a time when political and economic deregulation are the catchwords of the day, many co-operators have felt threatened. This is no wonder since co-operation, generally, has been presented as an alternative to the market economy. However, in 1992 the ICA Congress found itself able to conclude that

> "The basic co-operative values - such as self-help and mutual assistence, liberty and voluntariness, equity and democracy - are identical with most of the general ideas underlying structural adjustment programmes. At the same time the reduction of government influence and control remove the main obstacles in the way of the development of self-reliant co-operatives" (ICA 1992a:186).

What is remarkable here is not that the ICA adapts to changing circumstances. But the way that this change is defended deserves some attention. Can the basic co-operative values and 'ethos' really be used to legitimate virtually everything and all the possible roles which co-operatives may assume as development vehicles?

Facing the challenges of today and promising that co-operatives - due to their ethos and superior values - are better equipped to tackle whatever development problem that hits the head-lines can serve as pep-talk to hesitant officials and members of the movement. These bold assertions may, however, also serve as a narcotic, keeping the missionary spirit alive but preventing a necessary critical assessment about what co-operatives actually can be expected to accomplish. When the traditional role of co-operatives as junior partners of the state is seriously questioned, the alleged superiority of co-operatives to protect the environment may represent a much needed life-raft for disillusioned officials to cling to. Hence, it is pointed out that "co-operative enterprise has to be driven by optimism" (Yearbook of Co-operative Enterprise 1993:*vii*).

However, that may not be enough. We rather need to arrive at a more realistic assessment of what local organizations actually *can* do in relation to development in the Third World. In the short perspective our findings may discourage some co-operative believers. However, in the longer perspective they may be constructive in so far as they can help promoters of co-operatives and other non-governmental local organizations to avoid wasting time and energy on problems that are better solved by other means. After all, optimism and devotion may be necessary but it is not all that is required.

In order to reach a more realistic assessment of the role and potential of NGOs in general, and co-operatives in particular, in relation to development, we will look briefly at what is already known in relation to the above mentioned objectives of co-operatives in the Third World. The remainder of this paper will therefore highlight the three subjects 'co-operatives and the poor', 'co-operatives and women' and 'co-operatives and the environment'. In order to avoid being accused of selecting 'negatively biased' literature, the material used is primarily taken from publications emanating from the 'movement' itself.

Co-operatives and the Poor.

Co-operatives have often been expected to be especially beneficial to the poor segments of Third World populations. There is no denial that much needs to be done to improve the lot of the Third World's poor, but the belief that co-operatives - or any other specific organizations - are *ideal* instruments to achieve this goal seems somewhat misconceived. Actually, in a comparative study of rural local organizations in the Third World, Esman and Uphoff (1988:195) found that "co-operatives as a type of local organization show up as particularly unsuccessful on relative improvements in access to services for the poor". One reason is the commonly schewed priorities in co-operative promotion with undue emphasis on values at the expence of practical extension. Münkner (1979), for example, found that

> "some of the most unsuccessful local organizations' training efforts have been found among the co-operatives, where there has been a great deal of emphasis on the philosophy and goals of co-operation, but not enough on the mechanics of making co-operatives operate effectively" (quoted from Esman & Uphoff 1988:229).

However, also other types of local organizations scored low on asset redistribution (*ibid.*) reflecting the fact that local organizations often tend to reinforce already existing socio-economic differences. As a matter of fact, a number of case studies reveal that NGOs aiming to improve the situation of the rural poors were unable to reach the poorest 10 - 30 percent of the population (Farrington & Lewis 1993).

There are several examples that co-operatives, in various places, have increased the poors' incomes and improved their access to various services. There are, however, few examples where co-operatives have enhanced the poors' relative situation. When this has occurred, these positive experiences tend to be rather small-scale and without the expected general impact. There are numerous examples of co-operative organizations in which the benefits have primarily gone to already wealthy segments or stratas. Indeed, this is the dominating picture. This has especially been the case when governmentally controlled co-operatives have been used to distribute subsidized credits and inputs in short supply. This kind of 'co-operatives' has usually been permeated by patron-client networks and used (indirectly at least) to co-opt local notables at the poors' expence.

Co-operatives in many - if not most - countries have been used to tax agriculture and producer prices (set by the state) have usually been low, resulting in farmers' reluctance to grow 'government crops' and/or mushrooming 'black market' transactions (Bibagambah 1991; Holmén 1991). As a rule it has been easier for the wealthier farmers to turn to the more profitable uncontrolled crops. Poorer farmers, on the other hand, have been stuck with the imposed 'co-operative' pricing and regulation system. Another problem common in official 'co-operatives' has been delayed payments for produce delivered. Peasants have therefore preferred private traders. Private traders, even if they pay less, pay on delivery and therefore the peasant can at least be sure to get what has been agreed (Gyllström 1991; Jirström 1989). In many cases it has not been economically justifiable for Third World peasants to use official, state controlled co-operatives as sales agents for their produce. It is therefore not surprising that, for example, more than a quarter of Uganda's rural co-operatives have been found 'dormant' (ICA-ROESCA 1992) or that the average survival rate of Kenyan rural co-operatives (1971-83) was as low as 72% (Gyllström 1991). It must, however, be mentioned that not only exogenously introduced co-operatives show a bad record in these respects (see *e.g.* Holdcroft (1982) on 'community development schemes' and Arn (1988) on 'rural works programmes').

Also when we talk about voluntary co-operatives, the expectation that co-operatives would primarily be an instrument for social and economic betterment for the the poor, seems to be founded more on hope than on empirical evidence. Münkner (1976) has tried to identify which rural groups or strata in the Third World that can be expected to benefit from independent local co-operatives. He first distinguishes between rich, relatively rich and poor peasants but then broadens these categories into rich/relatively rich and the relatively poor/poor/destitute. He found the concept of co-operation to be of little relevance for the rich or affluent segments of the rural population. Hence, the idea of co-operation would only attract the relatively rich. The term poor, he says, is also too general. Therefore, he also differentiates between the relatively poor (those able to make small savings but not earning enough to build up reserves), the real poor (persons living at subsistence level, having no capacity to make even small savings), and the destitute (persons having an income below subsistence level or no income at all).

Thus, between the rich and the 'real poor' there is a middle layer. Co-operatives, Münkner underlines, can be used to strengthen this middle layer by offering people from above subsistence level the chance to work their way up to the middle layer. For poorer groups, with no resources to pool, co-operatives do not represent a realistic type of organization. For these groups other means will be necessary. However, if the middle layer is co-operatively organized in genuine self-help organizations, this could release public resources and enable governments to concentrate their efforts on programmes explicitly directed towards the poor (*ibid.*).

But it is not only wealth that (directly) determines who it is that has a stake in voluntary co-operation. As Jirström (1989) points out, "a co-operative is a demanding type of organization". To run a co-operative requires a minimum level of market orientation and certain necessary skills in literacy, administration, accounting, market overview, etc. In many cases poverty goes hand in hand with illiteracy, subsistence oriented production, etc. Hence, co-operatives generally tend to serve a commercial peasant class which is already integrated into the market economy. As pointed out by Harvey *et. al.* (1979), functioning co-operatives are likely to be a feature of relatively advanced (monetized) agrarian systems and primary a response to the requirements of cash production, rather than designed to meet the needs of excluded or subsistence groups.

This reflects the general difficulty in lastingly improving the situation of the poor through local organization building, no matter whether this is attempted from above or from below. Every illness needs a special treatment and in the real world there are no miracle cures. Obviously, co-operatives and other local organizations cannot be expected to function as social elevators for those who have nothing to contribute. There is nothing wrong in trying to alleviate poverty but there is no single way to achieve this goal and there certainly is no single type of organization that is 'ideal' in this respect. Rather, a variety of measures have to be taken and different modes of organization used. Local organizations can help some but they can not benefit all. To declare that, for example, co-operatives are especially suitable to benefit the Third World's poor may temporarily strengthen some western co-operative aid-givers' belief in the 'idea of co-operation' - but will it last when no proof can be presented? If not, it may be a relief to find a new problem for which the sacred organization is the 'ideal' solution - for example women's emancipation.

Cooperatives and Women.

It is obvious that the social and economic position of women needs to be strengthened in most parts of the world. Promotors of co-operatives and other local organizations have declared that it is one of their objectives to contribute to this. Fifteen years ago it was thus declared that "it is of paramount importance to include women in co-operatives" (Rupena-Osolnik 1978).

This was a response to the United Nations' proclamation of the international Women's Year 1975 and the 'Women's Decade' 1976-1985. The ICA was not slow to adopt this slogan. In 1975 it was thus stated that although the co-operative societies generally had not put the principle of equality between the sexes into practice (Räikkönen 1975:8), and in spite of the fact that "very few women reach the top positions in co-operatives (Seminck 1975:31), the "International Co-operative Movement ... is indeed in a position to help towards achieving the targets set up by the UN for 1975" (Räikkönen 1975:9). As Russel (1975:33) pointed out, it was no "coincidence that the first full working year of the ICA Women's Committee [was] concurrent with International Women's Year".

The 'Regional Conference on the Role of Women in Co-operative Development' held in Kuala Lumpur 1975, marks the starting point for this (then) newfound co-operative emphasis on women. It noted that women previously had "not been represented in the ... movement in numbers proportionate to their contributions" (ICA 1980:295). There are many explanations for this, usually reflecting women's traditionally inferior - if not outright exploited - position in most societies and cultures. However, the conference choose to blame this situation on the women themselves. The conference stated that "the greatest obstacle to women's participation is their lack of education in the co-operative principles and practices" (*ibid.*). Again, therefore, it was the 'sacred principles' and the 'superior ethos' that would improve the situation and extend the roles of women in society.

In 1980 the ICA Regional Office for South East Asia noted that "the role of women in co-operatives has not been ... significant" (ICA 1980:*ix*). The same report also suggested that the new focus on women could act "as a starting point of revitalization to a movement which was drifting in the doldrums" (*ibid:xi*). One may therefore question the motives behind this sudden interest in the previously overlooked one half of the world's population. Was the fundamental objective to improve the situation of women or was it just to find "ways in which women co-operators can contribute to the work of the Cooperative Movement"? (D'Cruz 1975:13). These two objectives are not necessarily the same.

In any case, it was soon reported that the newborn effort to integrate women in co-operatives and development had achieved "considerable success" (Meghi 1985). Others, however, are less inclined to second that conclusion. Grönberg and Johansson (1988:12), for example, bluntly stated that "it does not seem as if the Women's Decade has meant much for the integration of women into the development process".

Sometimes it has been stressed that women, as a rule, should be encouraged to participate more actively in already existing co-operatives. On other occasions it has been argued that since existing societies are male-dominated, women would generally benefit more if special co-operatives for women were established. All we can say here is that there is hardly a standard solution to this dilemma. In any case, since the declaration of the 'Women's Development Decade', funds are available and programmes for women are commonplace. Likewise, "most of the international organizations concerned with co-operatives are active in the question of women's participation" (Eastwood 1993). However,

> "many co-operative development schemes are [still] strongly donor-oriented. Instead of allowing prospective co-operators to form co-operative groups and to set the targets for their joint action themselves, politicians, development planners and donor representatives tend to set targets and to select target groups for their programmes or projects" (Münkner 1992a:264).

This is a reflection of the old-fashioned and paternalistic view that local organizations primarily constitute intermediaries or 'delivery systems' between the state and the local community (UN 1970, 1974; Kirsch *et. al.* 1980; Esman & Uphoff 1988) and that "co-operatives merely provide a useful forum through which the various social workers and experts can reach the rural populations and educate them in [various] matters" (Opondo 1975:15). Therefore, the fear has been expressed that women's "programmes could be in danger of being implemented where there is no real need" (Itkonen 1989), i.e. among easily accessible groups - relatively wealthy women who do not need to spend the whole day in the field - in relatively accessible areas. One may add that, with this top-down approach, there is also a danger that projects will not be initiated where there is a real need, i.e. among poorer strata and/or in remote locations. Reporting from Kenya (Sörensen 1990) found that while traditional (small and relatively insignificant) women's work- and saving-groups primarily attract the poorer women, registered (state supported) women's groups primarily reach the better off, married and middle-aged women.

A great problem for women's participation is that on many occasions "the woman did not even get the chance to become a member of a society, let alone fight for equality in that society" (Naali 1982:39). This is a common problem. In, for example, Africa and parts of Asia, where men usually are registered as land owners but women traditionally do most agricultural work, it is commonly the case that legislation or by-laws (requiring land ownership as a prerequisite for membership) prevents women from joining co-operatives (ILO 1988). Hence, women are at best 'shadow members' in existing societies or, where women's groups exist, these are "not registered as co-operatives" (*ibid*.).

Women, however, are not totally excluded but they face certain problems not affecting men. Extension officers, who are mostly males, tend to bypass women and disseminate agricultural information and advice only to male heads of households. Extension agents are trained to give advice about men's cash-crops but give little attention to women's food-crops (Grönberg & Johansson 1988). At the same time women extension agents, which are not as numerous, are predominantly trained in home economics (*ibid*.). The result is that "the orientation of women's projects ... reinforces women's traditional role" and has often "implied the segregation of women to jobs in a low-paid sector such as handicrafts, in contrast to the higher paid jobs favourable to men" (Borger-Poulsen 1985:178; see also Potivongsajarn 1993).

Where women are accepted as members in mixed and/or registered societies, their membership may actually increase their burden. In a case-study from Nicaragua, Yih (1991:35f) found that while men continued to dominate the co-operative "more women worked in co-operative agriculture than they had done previously, but [it] ... meant extra work for them rather than an opportunity to become more autonomous" (see also Monimart 1989). Generally, women have been found to "demonstrate better performance than men, especially in questions of thrift and in repayment of loans at the due date" (Eastwood 1993:142). While women here and there are "slowly working their way into the administrative positions in the co-operative structure... they are not active at policy making levels" (*ibid*:139). As a matter of fact, "women not only participate less but also seem to benefit less. They are acknowledged to be better savers but they do not have as much access to loans" (Potivongsajarn 1993:174; see also Meghi 1985).

Women, thus, tend to be discriminated against in mixed local organizations and co-operative societies. In a comparative study of various types of local organizations, Monimart (1989) found not only that women participate more but decide less and have less information. What is more important, she found no difference in approach towards women between the various agents (bilateral, multilateral or NGOs) supporting local organization building. This suggests that special women's groups and/or special co-operatives for women would benefit women more. A further argument in favour of special women's groups is that "men generally object to their wives or daughters moving around as single women [in mixed societies] because they fear that the women will have sexual affairs with other men. Hence, men seem to have much less against women's extra-domestic activities if they are organized within the framework of one or another form of women's groups" (von Bülow 1990:15).

However, even when so organized, women are under pressure to comply with established norms and expectations regarding proper behaviour. Hence, it is often the case that "women's organizations preserve women's realities, rather than transforming them" (Sörensen 1990:4). Esman and Uphoff (1988) found that while women are often excluded or consigned to minor or inconspicuous roles in mixed local organizations, all-female composition does neither favour empowerment, nor women's economic and social benefits.

This is not to say that co-operatives and women's groups do not benefit women. On the contrary, there are numerous examples of co-operative efforts which have improved the situation and broadened the roles of women. As it seems, however, these examples have been small-scale, local initiatives with limited impact (see, for example, Holmén 1989). Generally, they have improved the situation for women but they have not changed already established sex-roles and social structures. That would also have been to expect too much. To integrate women in development, to change their roles in society and to alter their general situation is an ardous and long-term project. It needs concerted action on many fronts and a variety of means are required. It is also questionable whether it is possible to change the roles of women by introducing a new form of organization. Womens' roles, rather, are likely to be altered as a function of development - if and when it 'takes off'. This will also be reflected in achievments and performance of both mixed local organizations and special women's groups.

Co-operatives and the Environment.

Environmental problems are different in different parts of the world. In the rich countries they are primarily related to inappropriate modern production techniques and 'over-development', resulting in conspicious consumption, growing waste mountains and air, soil and water pollution. In the poor countries, environmental problems are primarily caused by poverty, both at the national and the individual level. Inadequate - or even non-existent - waste- and pollution-control are increasingly severe problems in the Third World and some governments have even accepted foreign (western) dumping of hazardous waste as it gives an income in the short perspective. The Third World's major environmental problems, however, are in the form of land-degradation. In rural areas over-population and under-development force people to farm marginal and even sub-marginal lands, to over-extract soil, forests and groundwater reserves. Other environmental problems in the Third World are related to ill-managed irrigation schemes and deficient extension services, resulting in, for example, inappropriate use of fertilizers, insecticides, and herbicides. Hence, to combat environmental degradation will require a variety of approaches and it is questionable whether one type of organization can be the "best and most appropriate institution" to tackle these diverse problems.

It is sometimes stressed that co-operatives in various countries are engaged in reafforestation projects in areas threatened by desertification, that they utilize waste materials to produce electricity (ICA 1990a) and introduce locally produced solar energy (Prakash 1992; Holmén 1989). However, "in the co-operative sector not much has been done to conserve energy or to utilize or exploit other sources of energy" (Prakash 1992:12). It has also been found that "extension programmes for farmers' education through co-operative system about the efficient use of fertilisers and integrated nutrient management [are] not in vogue" (*ibid*:8). In fact, reporting from a study of 'co-operatives and the environment' in Asia, Prakash found that

> "initiative is lacking and co-operatives tend to 'shirk' their responsibilities [and] ... although co-operative education and training structures exist in the covered countries, no special efforts have been made to include environment-related topics in the curricula intended for ordinary co-operative members, co-operative employees and co-operative leaders" (*ibid*:14).

The situation is likely to be similar in other parts of the Third World. In fact, it may even be worse. In various countries, *e.g.* Kenya and Egypt, state supported co-operatives have been established in ecologically marginal areas (Gyllström 1991; Holmén 1991). Not only are they generally ineffective as far as productivity and members' incomes are concerned, but they are also actually - as for example the Ujamaa scheme in Tanzania (Shao 1986) - or potentially damaging to the physical environment in which they operate. What, then, can we expect from co-operatives in relation to environmental protection? Not so very much it seems.

The seriousness of the matter is likely to favour top-down approaches and increased central control of local activities. However, experience tells us that top-down approaches do not work. It has therefore been underlined that "many environmental problems can not be solved without the active participation of local people" (WDR 1992:93). However, it has also been found that "public participation has its drawbacks. Extensive participation ... can delay decision-making and participatory approaches tend to be expensive" (*ibid.*). Moreover, "decentralization of decision-making can easily reinforce the power of local elites" (*ibid*:95f). And these élites are often those least in need to engage in environmental protection (see below).

A further problem in relation to soil conservation measures is that most programmes are directed towards men since they, generally, are the formal land owners. However, the role of women in fighting desertification, etc. is crucial since they are often the real agriculturalists. Women remain permanently on the land while men, often, do not. In large parts of rural Africa men migrate, more or less permanently, to find work in urban areas. In Asia men often migrate for work in other countries, for example in the oil-economies in the Middle East. Not only is it, therefore, more difficult for men to decide on, let alone contribute to, protective measures - since they have other sources of income, men are less in need to do so. For women, on the other hand, "combatting desertification is the way forward to improve their living conditions, keep the men at home and prepare for their children's future" (Monimart 1989:15).

But it is not only a matter of adressing the proper target group. Blaikie (1985) found that governmental programmes for soil conservation often fail. He also found that the well-to-do (including politicians and senior bureaucrats) are not, generally, directly affected by soil erosion. Where they are, they also have the means to protect themselves against its effects. In many instances, the poor cannot afford protective measures due to lack of resources and the generally low discount rate of investments in conservation projects. As a matter of fact, they often cause soil erosion because they have no alternatives. Both co-operation and soil protection among this group is difficult. Still, Blaikie says, co-operative ventures in soil conserving land use and erosion works do have a role to play. However, such projects are "slow to show results" (p155) and their success tends to be "short-lived or small-scale" (p154). They "cannot ever hope to become the 'answer' to conservation since they tend to run counter to all [local and central] powerful interests" (p156). Blaikie is generally pessimistic about the future of the environment in LDCs and the poorer people who use it. He concludes that all we can realistically hope for is "a new intellectual approach and individual action - something which, by its own method, is deemed not to be enough" (*ibid*:157). There is much to support this conclusion, but maybe the situation is not so hopeless after all?

In recent years the co-operatively organized, non-governmental Naam movement in Burkina Faso has received great attention for its successful efforts to improve members' incomes while at the same time conserving soil, water and forests. Initiated in 1967, the Naam movement now has more than 200 000 members in Burkina Faso alone. It has also spread to neighbouring countries. However, in spite of successes, the movement suffers from lack of funds, mobilization problems, insufficient literacy and book-keeping skills and difficulties to spread information vertically and horizontally (Toburn 1992). Hence, in spite of all positive attention given to the Naam movement, it seems as if Blaikie's pessimistic conclusion is confirmed.

Similarly, Loiske's findings (1991) in a case-study of social stratification, attitudes to land management and soil conservation practices in a Tanzanian village show two things. First, that co-operation (voluntary, not superimposed) can be used to protect the environment and, second, that we should be careful with how far we stretch our expectations about what co-operation can contribute in this respect. In the investigated village, Loiske found a close relationship between land degradation and wealth as well as poverty. But he also found a group of farmers with some, but limited, resources - a middle layer (c.f. Münkner above) - who make conscious attempts to establish sustainable production systems on their farms.

In the investigated village the majority of villagers live in considerable poverty and lack both resources and incentives for proper land management. They are often indebted to the wealthier strata and in the pre-harvest period they often live in a state of semi-starvation. Not all of the poor farm their land which, moreover, is often marginal. Those among the poor who do cultivate their land cannot afford to use improved seeds, fertilizers or pesticides and, sometimes, not even use manure. The poor majority, thus, is forced to resort to soil-mining. It is common for poor land owners to rent out their holdings to a rich farmer and work as day labourers for him on their own fields. Such arrangements tend to enhance soil deterioration.

The rich farmers are only partly dependent on agriculture. They often own real estate and engage in trade and their economic activities stretch far outside the village. This is the most 'land hungry' group of villagers. They both 'invade' and cultivate common grazing areas and lease land from poor villagers. They cultivate with care the land that they own (land ownership is legally restricted) but heavily exploit rented land, the soil of which degrades in a short time. To them, this is no big problem as there is good supply of land for rent and as there still remain invadeable common grazing areas.

The middle layer, on the contrary, have no or few sources of income other than farming. These peasants depend on the land they own and rent little or no additional land. Therefore they "are anxious to check erosion and to maintain soil fertility" (Loiske 1991:11). They also have some resources to do this but these resources are limited. Therefore, "they often own means of production together, they co-operate to rear cattle and they work together during peak periods in agriculture" (*ibid*:8). In so doing they are able to maintain the quality of their land but, due to the large size of their families, they still face the risk of becoming empoverished. Hence, their land is not 'safe'. It is also an open question which impact their co-operative work methods and land conservation concerns will have on the other categories of land users. Obviously, it is more than education that is needed and under present conditions not all farmers seem to have reason to conserve soil.

Protecting the environment through co-operatives and other local organizations is thus a much more complicated task than generally acknowledged. It is not only a matter of educating extension agents and adressing the proper target groups, even if these are indeed important matters. Large segments of the rural population either are not directly affected by land degradation or are without means to protect the soil. The poor, who are most in need of protective measures, are generally the most difficult to reach and mobilize in local organizations. Most likely, therefore, environmental protection organized 'from below' is likely to be insufficient. This enhances the likelihood of coercive measures but coercion and top-down management has hitherto, in most cases, resulted in cheating, withdrawal and antigovernment sentiments - something many Third World governments can hardly afford.

Summary and Conclusions

Based on both theoretical considerations and general experience, we are now in a better position to make statements about what co-operatives can do about development and environmental protection in the Third World. The focus in this paper has been on co-operatives but the findings are relevant for other local organizations as well.

It is quite clear that people need to co-operate in various ways and at various levels to tackle the different problems of environmental degradation. If we/they do not try to overcome the environmental challenge together, the damage already done to nature may be irrepairable. That, however, is not the same thing as saying that co-operatives -- or, for that matter, any other type of NGO/LO -- are the 'best' instruments in this struggle or that they are 'ideally placed' to realize sustainable development. Our findings rather suggest that they are not.

The members of Third World co-operatives are mostly farmers and often relatively poor as well. As a rule they are poorly educated, often semi-literate and they generally lack information. Furthermore, they usually have few or no alternative ways of earning a living. For large segments of the Third World's rural population, lack of means and short-time survival strategies prevent long-term protective measures individually and collectively - even when it is known that they are necessary. Sometimes, however, the relatively poor farmers of the Third World do co-operate in, for example, reafforestation projects and/or take other measures to preserve the land they live and work on. But as a rule such joint actions are only likely to have limited impact.

In large degree, therefore, local organization building needs external support. But external support may turn out to be a double-edged sword, often leading to aid-dependency and/or passivity. "Governments and donor organizations need a certain degree of organization in order to reach out to recipients with knowledge and material support; recipients have to be organized in order to receive and, in the opinion of some governments and donors, in order to participate in the development process" (Arn 1988:1). However, for a number of reasons it has proved persistently difficult to enhance the socio-economic position of the poor who, due to their numbers, are a crucial group to mobilize for protective measures. Likewise, women - an equally crucial category - (which, in many cases, can not be separated from the poor) have often been neglected or bypassed as members of local organizations. They are accepted as members but often have little influence on activities. In this connection no great differences seem to exist between different types of local or external, supporting organizations.

State supervised co-operatives, sofar, have usually been hampered by paternalism and members' indifference or mistrust. It is likely that paternalism will increase if such parastatals are to enforce protective land conservation measures. The result would then, most likely, be even less efficiency. Extension agents in such organizations, further, tend to be insufficiently educated in environmental protection and if they are assigned protective tasks too abruptly, there is an obvious risk that they may do more harm than good.

It is thus an illusion to believe that when the "ICA calls upon its 625 000 000 individual members to continue the battle for environmental protection" (ICA 1990:77; 1992:190), "all members of the co-operative world [will automatically] stand together to participate in this most important activity of our life time, *i.e.* protecting the environment" (ICA 1992:191). If it is believed - even within the 'movement' - that 'co-operators of the world' can be commandeered to 'stand together' every time a major problem is gaining world-wide attention, then that actually reveals a fundamental misconception about what co-operation is all about!

What co-operative organizations *can* do is to lobby local and central governments, to increase information campaigns and, especially, to devote more efforts to the education of members, employees and elected representatives on all levels about environmental protection. These are necessary steps to take. But the task is enormous and not likely to show quick, tangible results. It is, never the less, of paramount importance that the rich countries direct aid-money to education of extension agents, farmers, etc. on environmental matters. It is equally important, however, that the common peasant's often superior knowledge of his local environment is respected and taken into account. Otherwise educational campaigns are likely to fail. Co-operative aid-agencies and western promotors of co-operation in the Third World are now beginning to include analyses of environmental consequences of their various aid-programmes and projects. It is extremely important that such analyses are extended and institutionalized - provided they are based on realism rather than on hope.

The contribution of informal co-operation by Third World peasants and by the more institutionalized co-operative organizations to environmental protection, forest, soil and water conservation, etc. can at best be expected to be slow, limited and not enough. This is so also for other types of NGOs. But it *is* a contribution. Other organizations, hopefully, will make their contributions as well. But none is likely to be ideal or most appropriate to solve 'most if not all problems of development'. Promotors of development in the Third World ought to avoid making such ill-founded declarations.

Presently the ICA, together with its various regional and specialized organs, is lobbying to convince the UN to declare 1995 as the 'International Year of Co-operatives' (Pirson 1989). If that is to be effectuated, it will not suffice to 'embrace co-operation with optimism' or for representatives of the movement to urge each-other to 'believe in what they are doing'. Before an 'International Year of Co-operation' can be declared not so few promotors of co-operation as an ideal development instrument must rid themselves of blinkers preventing them to arrive at a more down-to-earth appreciation of what co-operatives can be expected to accomplish in relation to the interrelated matters of poverty alleviation, women's liberation and environmental protection. At a time when the human habitat is more seriously threatened than ever before, dream-selling is not the answer. Promotors of co-operation must make up their minds. Is it sustainable development they want to realize, or is it "sustainable co-operative development" as it was expressed by the ICA (1992c)? In the latter case it would mean an enlarged - but largely indifferent - member cadre.

Presently an increasing amount of official aid money directed to the Third World is being channelled through various kinds of northern NGOs. Hence, the importance of public funding for the 'development' of northern NGOs increases. Both the numbers of northern NGOs and the competition among them about being selected as channels for "NGO-aid" increases as well. Therefore, it is likely that we will see more 'dream-selling', questionable marketing, misdirected lobbying, etc. in order to boost the image of all kinds of 'development promoting' NGOs. Whether this will improve aid effectiveness may be open to question. As mentioned in chapter one, the NGO approach is not necessarily a superior one.

Münkner (1992:92) has declared that the time has come for "co-operatives, national co-operative movements and the ICA as their worldwide apex organization [to arrive at] a clear vision of a common goal and of their future role in socio-economic development". With this I can only agree.

Furthermore, at a time when western development aid to the Third World is seriously and increasingly questioned, aid agencies -- among them promotors of Third World co-operatives -- are better advised to face reality and to make realistic assessments of what their contributions *can* be. Even if it is not so much, and even if they can not alleviate all problems, they can make important contributions. When aid efforts are directed towards *attainable objectives* and proper target groups, development aid may eventually become effective.

References:

Apthorpe R, Gasper D (1982): Policy Evaluation and Meta Evaluation: The Case of Rural Co-operatives. *World Development,* Vol 10, No 8. pp651-668.

Arn A-L (1988): *The Making of Institutions and Leaders at Rice Root Level: Inside the Rural Works Programme in Southern Bangladesh.* CDR Project Paper 88.3, Copenhagen, Center for Development Research.

Berger-Poulsen K (1985): Integration or Segregation - The Gap Between Good Intentions and Appropriate Actions in Africa. *Community Development Journal.* Vol. 20, No. 3, July. pp176-183.

Bibagambah J (1991): *Agricultural Merketing Intervention and Oricing Policies in Uganda.* Makerere University. mimeo.

Blaikie P (1985): *The Political Economy of Soil Erosion.* London & New York, Longman.

Bonow M (1969): *Demokratisk Ekonomi.* Uddevalla, Rabén & Sjögren.

Bülow von D (1991): *Perceiving Women's Worlds: Kipsigis women in Kenya.* CDR Working Paper 91.1, Copenhagen, Center for Development Research.

COPAC (1978): *Co-operatives Against Rural Poverty.* Report from a Symposium held at Vår Gård, Saltsjöbaden, Sweden, July 31 - Aug. 4, 1978. Rome, COPAC.

D'Cruz M (1975): Women's Co-operative Activities in S.E. Asia. *Review of International Co-operation.* Vol 68, No 1. pp10-13.

Dülfer E (1975): *Zur Krise der Genossenschaften in der Entwicklunspolitik.* Marburger Schriften zum Genossenschaftswesen. Reihe B/Band 10. Göttingen, Vandenhoeck & Ruprecht.

Eastwood T (1993): Promoting Women's Participation in Co-operatives. *Yearbook of Co-operative Enterprise 1993.* The Plunkett Foundation. pp139-142.

Esman MJ, Uphoff NT (1988): *Local Organizations - Intermediaries in rural development.* Ithaca and London, Cornell University Press.

Farrington J, Lewis DJ (1993): *Non-Governmental Organizations and the State in Asia.* London and New York, Routledge.

Grönberg E-B, Johansson M (1988): *Zambian Women and the Co-operative Movement - a Case Study of Nachikungu MPC Society Ltd.* Rapporter och Notiser Nr 85, Department of Social and Economic Geography, University of Lund.

Gyllström B (1991): *State Administered Rural Change - Agricultural Co-operatives in Rural Kenya.* London & New York, Routledge.

Harvey C, Jacobs J, Lamb G, Schaffer B (1979): *Rural Employment and Administration in the Third World.* ILO, Saxon House.

Hasselman E (1971): *Rochdaleprinciperna - de kooperativa idéernas historia.* Stockholm, Rabén & Sjögren.

Holdcroft LE (1982): 'The Rise and Fall of Community Development in Developing Countries 1950-65: A Critical Analysis and Implications.' In (Ed.) Jones & Rolls: *Progress in Rural Extension and Community Development.* John Wiley & Sons, New York, pp207-231.

Holmén H (1989): Basaisa, en by i Nildeltat - 8 år senare. *Geografiska Notiser* 1989:1, pp22-30.

Holmén H (1990): *State, Co-operatives and Development in Africa.* Research Report No. 86, The Scandinavian Institute of African Studies, Uppsala.

Holmén H (1991): *Building Organizations for Rural Development - State and Co-operatives in Egypt.* Lund, Lund University Press.

Holmén H, Öjermark P (1992): Past and Present Role, Progress and Problems of Co-operatives in Agricultural Marketing, Input Supply and Rural Credit, and Prospects for the Future. In: *Report from 'Nordic Workshop on Peasant Agricultural Marketing in Eastern Africa'. Appendix VIII.* Swedish University of Agricultural Sciences/IRDC, January 1992.

ICA (1978): *Report of an Experts' Consultation on Co-operatives and the Poor.* London, ICA.

ICA (1980): *Enhancing Women's Participation in Co-operative Activities.* New Delhi, ICA.

ICA (1990a): The Co-operative Movement and the Environment. *Review of International Co-operation.* Vol. 83, No. 2, pp79-98.

ICA (1990b): Co-operative Day Message. *Review of International Co-operation.* Vol. 83, No. 2, pp76f.

ICA (1992a): *Review of International Co-operation. (XXXth Congress Tokyo October, 1992. Agenda and Reports),* Vol. 85, No. 2/3 1992.

ICA (1992b): *ICA News. (Special Issue on the Environment).* No. 3:1992. Geneva, ICA.

ICA (1992c): Eds: Shrotriya & Prakash. *Environment and Co-operatives.* New Delhi, ICA.

ICA-ROESCA (1992): Uganda Co-operative Statute Discussed. *Co-op News,* Jan-June, pp3 and 5.

ILO (1988): *Co-operatives - A Review of Co-operative Development in the African Region: Scope, Impact and Prospects.* Seventh African Regional Conference, Harare, Nov-Dec. 1988. Geneva, ILO.

Itkonen R (1989): Women and Co-operatives. *Review of International Co-operation.* Vol 82, No 4. pp95-97.

Jirström M (1989): *Agricultural Co-operatives in Zimbabwe.* Rapporter och Notiser Nr 90. Institutionen för Kulturgeografi och Ekonomisk Geografi, Lunds Universitet.

Johansson TA (1980): A Brief History of Farmers' Organizations in Sweden. In: *Farmers' Co-operation in Sweden: Origins and Development.* Stockholm, LT:s Förlag. pp13-64; 133-135.

Karlander O (1981): Internationellt kooperativt samarbete är nödvändigt. In: *Imorgon kooperation - ett folkrörelsealternativ.* Stockholm, Kommundepartementet. pp148-177.

Kemppinen H (1992): Eka Corporation and the Environment. In: *ICA News (Special Issue on the Environment),* No 3:1992. Geneva, ICA, p10.

Kirsch O, Benjacov A, Schujmann L (1980): *The Role of Self-Help Groups in Rural Development Projects.* Saarbrücken/Fort Lauderdale, Breitenbach Publ.

Klöwer GG (1977): *Chancen von Genossenschaften in Entwicklungsländern. Chancen ihrer Entstehung und Chancen als entwicklungspolitisches Instrument gezeigt am Beispiel Ägyptens.* Marburg/Lahn, Phillips Universität.

Konopnicki M (1978): 'Introduction'. In: Konopnicki & Vandevalle (Eds): *Co-operation as an Instrument for Rural Development.* London, ICA/University of Ghent. pp7-11.

Loiske V-M (1991): *Who Has Reason to Conserve Soil? Lessons from Giting village, Tanzania.* EDSU Working Paper No. 12, Dept. of Cultural Geography, University of Stockholm.

Mabogunje A (1982): *The Development Process - A spatial perspective.* London, Unwin Hyman.

Marcus L (1988): *Kooperationen och dess grundläggande värderingar.* Stockholm, ICA.

Meghi Z (1985): Women and Co-operatives - Some Realities Affecting Development in Tanzania. *Community Development Journal.* Vol. 20, No. 3, July. pp185-188.

Monimart M (1989): *Women in the fight against desertification.* IIED Paper No. 12, December 1989.

Münkner HH (1976): *Co-operatives for the Rich or for the Poor?* Institute for Co-operation in Developing Countries. Marburg/Lahn.

Münkner HH (1992a): Co-operative Values and Development Aid. In: *Review of International Co-operation, (XXXth Congress Tokyo October, 1992. Agenda and Reports).* Vol 85, No 2/3. pp253-281.

Münkner HH (1992b): Possible ICA Development Strategy for the Next Decade. *Review of International Co-operation.* Vol 85, No 1. pp81-98.

Naali S (1982): Equality for Women in Co-operatives - Legislation and Reality. *Review of International Co-operation.* Vol 75, No 1. pp36-45.

Opondo DH (1975): Educational Activities for Women Co-operators in East Africa. *Review of International Co-operation.* Vol 68, No 1. pp14-17.

Pierce JT (1990): *The Food Resource.* Harlow, Longman.

Pirson (1989): 1995 - International Year of Co-operatives. *Review of International Co-operation.* Vol82, No 4, pp83f.

Potivongsajarn ZC (1993): Women and Co-operatives in Asia. *Yearbook of Co-operative Enterprise 1993.* The Plunkett Foundation. pp173-178.

Prakash D (1990): *A Place to Live - Roles Co-operatives can play in Protecting the Environment.* New Delhi, ICA.

Prakash D (1992): *Sustaining Environment Through Co-operative Action.* New Delhi, ICA.

Rupena-Osolnik M (1978): The Role of Women in the Agricultural Co-operative Movement. *Review of International Co-operation.* Vol 71, No. 1, pp43-49.

Russel MJ (1975): Promotion of World-wide Women's Co-operative Interests. *Review of International Co-operation.* Vol 68, No 1. pp33-36.

Räikkönen S (1975): Women and the Co-operative Movement. *Review of International Co-operation.* Vol. 68, No. 1. pp8f.

Seminck M-L (1975): Women's Participation in the Co-operative Movements of Western Europe. *Review of International Co-operation.* Vol. 68, No. 1. pp30-32.

Shao J (1986): The Villagization Program and the Disruption of the Ecological Balance in Tanzania. *Canadian Journal of African Studies.* Vol20, No 2, pp219-239.

Sörensen A (1990): *Women's Organizations and Changing Gender Relations Among the Kipsigis of Kenya.* CDR Project Paper 90.5, Copenhagen, Center for Development Research.

Toburn K (1992): 'The Naam movement in Burkina Faso'. *IDRCurrents* No. 4, October 1992. pp23-26.

UN (Economic and Social Council) (1970): *The Role of the Co-operative Movement in the Achievment of the Goals and Objectives of the Second United Nations Development Decade.*

UN (Economic and Social Council) (1974): *Contributions made by the Co-operative Movement to the Objectives of the Second United Nations Development Decade.*

UNRISD (1975): *Rural Co-operatives as Agents of Change: a Research Report and a Debate.* Geneva, UNRISD.

Yearbook of Co-operative Enterprise 1993. The Plunkett Foundation.

Young C, Sherman NP, Rose TH (1981): *Co-operatives and Development: Agricultural Politics in Ghana and Uganda.* Madison, The University of Wisconsin Press.

Chapter Three

Co-operatives as Instruments of Rural Development[1]

- The Case of India

By Neelambar Hatti and Franz-Michael Rundquist

Introduction

Cooperative organizations have been extensively used in Indian development planning[2] as a tool of promoting structural changes in several sectors, not least the agrarian sector. In two earlier papers[3] the authors have analyzed the role of cooperatives in promoting rural development in India.

However, our own studies, as well as the implications we draw from other studies dealing with cooperative development in the Third World, have convinced us of the need to further explore the problems involved in creating viable organizational structures to promote the pace and direction of rural development.

The present paper is divided into two sections. First, we focus our analysis on the environments in which an organization has to function. Second, against this background we will discuss the role of cooperatives in rural development as we see it in terms of our own research and other studies.

---

1 This paper was orignally published in Journal für Entwicklungspolitik, Vol. 9:4, 1993. The authors wish to express their gratitude to the Editorial Committee of JEP for the permission to also publish the paper in the present anthology.

2 See the various Indian Five Year Plans since 1951.

3 See Hatti, N. and Rundquist, F-M. (1989a and b).

Organizations and Rural Development

Rural development is a multi-dimensional process which involves extending the benefits of development to the rural poor. Gross inequality in land ownership and invidious institutional structure which sap initiative and incentive are among the most serious obstacles to rural development in developing countries (Chambers 1974, 1983; Hatti and Rundquist 1989b; Hill 1987). The prime constraints are structural, economic, technological and organizational. Of these, organizational barriers play a critical role in determining the pace of development.

Organizations constitute an important basis for rural transformation. Organizations can provide impulses for initiating and stimulating growth, and provide a forum for the participation of people in decision-making. They help establish group dynamics, identify common needs of people and provide a channel for the transfer of technology. Thus, organizations can be the focal point for decentralized planning and decision-making.

This would imply the involvement of various organizations to enhance such aspects as production, productivity and employment generation (cf. Chambers 1983, Harriss 1984, Johnston and Clark 1982, Lea and Chaudhri 1983). These include effective utilization of natural resources to increase production, processing and marketing, provision for infrastructure facilities and supporting services so as to improve the quality of life. Consequently, the term organization must have a broad connotation to encompass such factors as physical infrastructure, the delivery system, administration manpower and spatial planning (Dantwala 1980:53).

Organizational Environments

An important aspect pertaining to the roles and functioning of organizations concerns not only their structure but also the environments in which they operate.

> "One of the most common concerns in the literature on the place of local organizations in rural development is the extent to which their environment, broadly defined, affects or even determines their ability to perform effectively. Very often, the issues are framed in terms of the hindrances or barriers that

environmental factors may present. Hyden's analysis of cooperatives in East Africa (1973), for example, maintained that they were extremely weak vis-à-vis their sociopolitical environment and that their ineffectiveness was caused by their vulnerability to external manipulation." (Esman and Uphoff 1988:102).

The concept of environment as used in this paper refers to the totality of physical, social, economic and political influences affecting an organization, and also a notion of the extent to which these can be manipulated by an organization. Environment in this perception consists of several layers that are more or less apparent and influenceable. Elements of our conception of the environments surrounding an organization engaged in rural development activities are outlined in Figure 1.

Prior to discussing this figure, however, it is necessary to describe some of the more general tenets of the environmental conception. Three levels of environments can be defined - the *controlled, influenceable* and *appreciated* environments (cf. Gyllström 1991, Lorsch and Allen 1973, Smith et al. 1980, Thompson 1973).

The *controlled* environment comprises of one or several core activities whose composition and interrelationships to different degrees may be defined by formalized rules and administrative systems. The *influenceable* environment is made up of the physical resources and social actors being of direct consequence for the organizations and to which the organization has a reciprocal relationship - for example, arable land, institutions, input suppliers, marketing organizations and banks. Finally, the *appreciated* environment accommodates factors affecting organizational performance, but then factors generally outside the sphere within which they are subject to direct influences from the organization in question. Examples of the latter are - demographic characteristics of an organization's area of operation, health standards, educational levels, access to social infrastructure, transport-/communication networks, ecology, world market and/or other externally set prices.

Thus, an individual organization can be perceived as being linked to fields of interaction and influences composed of forces originating at local, regional, national and even international levels. Given the purpose of an organization, its behaviour can be seen as reflecting a mosaic of actions and reactions following from its relations to different facets of its environment.

Performance, of which *efficiency* is one aspect, would then reflect the extent to which this behaviour results in achievement of the organization's objectives. *Impact* would indicate an organization's influences on the social, economic and physical aspects of its environments in relation to more generally defined criteria or objectives.

With this perspective it is possible to return to Figure 1 and explore the ways in which the different environments impact on a given organization. The three environments are shown by way of rectangles of different sizes that are further subdivided into different sub-segments. The two rectangles in the centre of the figure primarily represent the *controlled* and *influenceable* environments, although some aspects of what we call the appreciated environment by necessity are also included. Surrounding these, in the peripheral layer, is represented the *appreciated* environment.

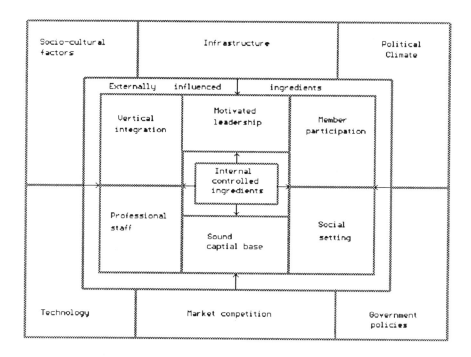

Figure 1: Organizational environments

The centre of *Figure 1* can be said to represent the very core of organizational activities. That different types of organizational structures are externally imposed, and frequently given monopolies within certain sectors of the local economies is well known. Still, even if the organizations are subject to detailed controls, there is always some leverage left for local initiatives, and this is indicated by the *"Internal controlled ingredients"*. In terms of activity orientation these could, for example, comprise of details of credit giving procedures, investment plans, and decisions on compulsory member workdays (cf. i.a. Hedlund 1986). Depending on the extent of external controls imposed, the range of responsibility left to local management may vary substantially from country to country, and even within countries on a regional basis.

However, no organization can exist and function in a vacuum. Hence, organizationally specific decisions will be conditioned by various factors in its area of operation, as illustrated by the middle rectangle and the six sub-segments into which this one is subdivided. Of these, the two most obvious are *"Motivated leadership"* and *"Membership participation"*. Linked to these one also finds *"Professional staff"*. All three are important for properly functioning local organizations, and deficiencies in one or several of these respects have often led to apparent failures of otherwise well intentioned rural development projects.

In terms of organizational environments, these factors could be seen as primarily belonging to the influenceable environment. As indicated, however, the influence exerted is based on a reciprocal relationship with the controlled environment. Hence, the need-fulfilment function of an organization is probably the most important determinant of both a motivated leadership and high membership participation. If perceived as satisfying essential local needs high participation rates are expected. Also, local leadership should be more highly motivated in fulfilling organizational goals. In addition, a high degree of membership participation puts pressure on leaders and staff to properly exercise their respective roles.

Remaining segments in the middle rectangle are *"Social setting"*, *"Capital base"*, and *"Vertical integration"*. Social setting and vertical integration to a large extent fall under the appreciated environment and are only to a limited extent controlled/influenced by the individual organization. In terms of goal fulfilment, however, both factors are important. The extent to which organizational goals are compatible with those of the society in which the organization operates, naturally, affects organizational efficiency. Also, vertical integration - frequently manifested through externally imposed organizational structures[4] - largely belong to the appreciated environment and is only to a limited extent influenceable by a local organization. The extent to which this structure is compatible with local goals will strongly influence organizational impact and efficiency.

Finally, the capital base, obviously, forms the foundation for a properly functioning local organization. To a large extent this factor is found within the influenceable sphere of an organization, and is very much linked to motivated leadership and professional staff. At the same time, externally imposed demands or infringements of operational freedoms may negatively influence potential goal fulfilment. Hence, content and structure of the links between an organization, its influenceable and appreciated environments are critical for the proper functioning of the organization. Unfortunately, a lot of research (cf. i.a. Gyllström and Rundquist 1989) indicates that these links more often than not tend to circumscribe and restrict goal fulfilment rather than being supportive in their operations.

Lastly, the outer rectangle consists of six sub-segments, which basically represent the appreciated environment. To degrees, however, some of the factors indicated fall within the sphere of the controlled environment - particularly infrastructure, technology and, to a lesser degree, socio-cultural factors. In a broader perspective, though, the possible impact on these factors by the type of rural development organizations generally found in the Third World, can only be marginal. The implication is that large sectors of importance for organizational functioning and efficiency are beyond their immediate control, and that these are heavily dependent on policies of external bodies.[5]

---

4 For example, the common hierarchical organization of cooperatives from an apex organization over unions down to individual societies with different powers and responsibilities assigned to each level.

5 Primarily governmental bodies at national and sub-national levels.

Organizational Development

The success of any organization implementing a developmental strategy ultimately depends not only upon proper mobilization of local resources in men and material, but more specifically on its ability to involve the local population in the process. However, a major weakness in the official strategy has been that the responsibility of planning and implementing local development programmes has rested in the hands of bureaucratic agencies or organizations sponsored by the State. Rarely have the people for whom the efforts at improving their lives been given any responsibility in these processes. Nor have these organizations properly utilized local material resources. Needless to say, an externally imposed *"Blueprint Approach"* (Hydén 1983) alone cannot bring about a meaningful integration of people and organizations. The benefits of State sponsored rural development programmes hitherto have largely accrued to the top economic and social strata who could manipulate the responsible agencies (Dasgupta 1984, Holmén 1991).

Broadly, efficiency of rural organizations depends upon two sets of factors; rural power structures and government policies. These are internal as well as external in character, and the interplay of these factors determines the emergence, development and performance of rural organizations.

Key elements in organization building in rural settings are leadership, doctrine, education and environment. In India, after independence, several attempts were made to tackle the rural problems through institutional approaches. Evolution of *community development blocks*, *cooperatives* and *panchayats* were the main instruments for rural development during the fifties. *Community development blocks*, however, became bureaucratic institutions. Moreover, people's participation in the affairs of cooperatives and panchayats was marginal on account of the social and economic dualism that perpetuated the rural power polity.

The introduction of the *Intensive Agriculture District Programme (IADP)* in the early sixties gave new stimulus to agricultural growth. The emphasis here was for raising production of field crops by means of appropriate production techniques, and the necessary organizational support to accomplish this was also set up. This approach helped in shattering the popular myth that the Indian farmer was conservative and backward looking. However, this programme generally benefited the larger, better educated, and more influential sections of the peasantry in irrigated tracts. The outcome was the adoption of an *'elitist'* model in rural development.

For dry regions, a similar programme known as the *Intensive Agriculture Area Programme (IAAP)* was launched. Close on the heels came the seed-fertilizer revolution in the late sixties. It triggered off what came to be known as the *"Green Revolution"* which, even though region specific, boosted food output and brought an era of plenty. In all these programmes a package philosophy was the basic concept.

Since the 1970s several attempts have been made to improve the incomes of the rural poor through *ad hoc* measures - *Drought Prone Area Programme (DRAP), Small and Marginal Farmers' Development Programme (SFDA), Command Area Development Programme (CADP), Food for Work Programme (FWP) and Antyodaya*[6] are examples of the isolated efforts made. These attempts have not had the desired impact for lack of suitable organizational frameworks that link resources, people and the state.

A more comprehensive strategy known as the *Integrated Rural Development Programme (IRDP)* was introduced in the Sixth Five Year Plan. This programme focused on a sectoral- and special integration of activities under the *District Rural Development Agency*. However, here again, the absence of an integration between men and materials through a localized institutional agency resulted in delusions and mistakes in implementation.

These and other beneficiary oriented, subsidized programmes have compounded the concentration of powers and patronage, enhancing the mis-delivery of benefits to the unintended. What is conspicuous in these programmes is the absence of the role and participation of the people - either in planning and implementation or raising of local resources. Jain et al. (1985:110) write:

> "Thus, /.../, the various strategies adopted so far have been basically similar as they are anti-people and anti-development. So, strategies which did not work in the past, are not working at present, and can hardly be expected to work in the future."

---

6 This programme refers to *"the upliftment of the poorest of the poor"* and was introduced during the sixth plan. See, Programme Evaluation Organization (1978).

On the whole, state efforts for rural development do not appear to have had much positive impact.[7] It frequently lacks the strategy and design for development focused on the specific objective of activating the human factor in the rural economy. Programmes have usually been designed to operate only as delivery systems, and a delivery system - even an efficient one - cannot quite overcome the barriers in rural development. State policies will have to consider new ways of promoting social and economic integration in order to become active instruments for the emergence of viable rural communities. As a part of this work, state policy has to concern itself with the revitalization of existing institutions such as, for example, the panchayats in India, and cooperatives. Most importantly, state polices need to have a design to strengthen the position of the local economies *vis-a-vis* the larger national economy (cf. Chopra et al. 1990). Without such a design, state intervention will remain just a delivery system and not a force capable of bring about needed changes (Rao 1983:689).

Integrated Strategy

On the whole, the efforts in India to bring about changes in rural areas have not been a great success due to many in-built rigidities in the organizational set-up.

> "The agency which urges him (farmer) to change may not itself be capable of effecting the needed environmental change smoothly nor giving the needed advices which are made by officials (or foreign advisers), and he is naturally not willing to risk too much. His experience of government efficiency is not after all favourable" (Hunter 1971:111).

In rural development processes, directions should be clear, goals identified and the *modus-operandi* employed should involve the villagers. It needs an institutional set-up that can integrate multiple goals. This would call for a kind of *'systems approach'* in organizational pursuits.

---

7 Even the more recent programmes such as Jawahar Rozgar Yojana (JRY), which was aimed at creating rural employment, have not been successful.

Integrated development would, then, demand taking into account in the planning and implementation process not only the local material resources but more so the economic and social resources of a community. *"The overall concern should be one of community orientation, minimum state intervention, mass participation, non-specialization, pooling of the local resources and services to the people"* (Varma and Pillai 1980:86).

This would require a strong base level institution. For obvious reasons, such an agency should have the consent of the people and must be nourished by them. An institution that can work on the basis of decentralized authority, and a centralized information system - controlled by the decentralized authority, but not under government control - could be the most appropriate one (Desai and Prakash 1974:154).

Furthermore, any agency involved in planning for rural development should be prepared to make arrangements for providing the participants with the necessary prerequisites for optimally utilizing the planned facilities (Srivastava et al. 1975:277). The relevance of an activity should be the criterion for the selection of an area for the implementation of a programme. Failures of the government machinery to forge effective linkages between various interest groups in rural areas, however, has strengthened the case for voluntary action through institutional structures (cf. Gohlert 1987, Srivastava et al. 1975).

> "We have to bring about that blend of voluntary initiative and bureaucratic action which can generate the enthusiasm required to deliver the goods without waste and misdirection of resources" (Nair 1981:40).

Thus, in the final analysis only organizations promoted by people themselves can initiate and sustain development processes.

Co-operatives and Rural Development

In India, the aims of rural development policies have been to find suitable forms of organizations for the dissemination of production credits and the provision of marketing outlets for needed agricultural inputs. In this context, cooperatives have been assigned a central role, and have in some areas become important focal points for banking, sales of consumer goods, and the dissemination of more general types of development credits. To varying degrees cooperatives have also become important marketing channels for parts of the agricultural surplus production. Not all types of crops are marketed through cooperatives, though, and the latter function mainly refers to more subsistence oriented crops. In effect, rural based cooperatives have frequently become *multi-purpose cooperatives* taking on a number of supporting functions for the transformation and development of the agrarian sector, as well as supporting functions for a more general rural development process.

Cooperative rural development policies in other Third World countries bear many similarities to the policies pursued in India. Variations in their concrete manifestations, organization, and functioning may exist, but the dominant impression is one of similarity rather than difference.

Although examples of well functioning cooperatives do exist, the overwhelming impression is that cooperative organizations in India, and elsewhere, have not been successful in promoting rural development (cf. Apthorpe 1972; Hatti and Rundquist 1989a and b; Hedlund 1986; Holmén 1991, Hydén 1980; Gyllström 1989, 1991). Their performance records are often plagued with failures and, seen in longer perspectives, replete with information on liquidated societies (cf. Gyllström 1991).

Two main tendencies become apparent. First, and foremost, cooperative organizations have failed in promoting a broadly based rural development process. Intended services and benefits have frequently been *"appropriated"* by the already wealthy and influential members of the target communities. Hatti and Rundquist (1989a), for example, concluded that:

> "...as indicated, the cooperatives in Sirsi Taluk seem more geared towards meeting the needs of landowners, particularly those producing garden crops, and, as a consequence of the social stratification, more geared towards serving the needs of the traditionally wealthy and economically powerful groups of the society." (Hatti and Rundquist 1989a:124).

Papers presented at a workshop in New Delhi on cooperatives and rural development in India confirm that while cooperatives have played a positive role in agricultural development, the services extended are not enjoyed equally. Thus, cooperatives have widened inequalities.

> "Though the formal ownership of the cooperative is democratic, in actual practice large growers control its policies /..../ the dominance of the

economically privileged coterie is mainly due to two factors. Firstly, they are able to intimidate the small growers by the sheer weight of their ownership. Secondly, they use their links with the government to establish a *patron-client relationship* which prevents democratic functioning." (Our emphasis) (Jain et al. 1985:57).

Along a similar vein with respect to a Minimum Needs Programme in drought-prone areas in India it has also been observed that:

"Given the existing structure of rural societies, the benefits of this service have been mainly to the advantage of farmers already with access to productive resources. The present set-up has not been able to cope with the built-in power relations." (Bengtsson 1979:13).

These observations overlap with conclusions drawn by several other authors concerned with organizational aspects of rural development (cf. Attwood and Baviskar 1988; Hydén 1980, 1983; Mars 1986; Robertson 1984; Sandbrook 1985; UNDP 1984). Recurrent arguments are that development problems are socio-political in origin and based on ethnic conflicts, clan politics, regional and religious factionalism. Interpretations come close to the *'tradition versus modernity'* perspective as it has frequently been discussed in the African context (Hydén 1983). Modern institutions are perceived as alien, and newly introduced roles of social and economic interactions do not conform to moral obligations based on prevailing cultural values.

Second, concerning the relatively successful cooperatives, it can be noted that these share some common traits such as economic self-interest that tend to set them apart from the broad mass of cooperatives found in the Third World. They are frequently more geared towards being producer or *'monoculture'* cooperatives - as opposed to being multi-purpose cooperatives - focusing on a single cash-crop. Over time a tendency towards widening the range of services provided is often observed, but their main emphasis continues to be the productive activities for which they were once started. They also tend to operate in areas that are ecologically, infrastructurally, and otherwise, well suited for the types of activities engaged in. In addition, their areas of operation tend to be relatively homogeneous and well defined in terms of both ecological preconditions and social and economic differentiation among their target populations (Gyllström 1991; Hedlund 1986; Mascharenas 1988).

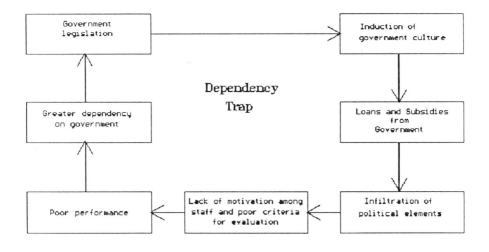

Figure 2: The vicious circle of state-initiated cooperatives/local organizations

The obvious relation between economic self-interest and organizational development can be derived from the general observation that cooperative/rural organizations are instruments of joint efforts among people aiming at achieving a common goal, and for the fulfilment of private goals members would not be able to attain on their own. This involvement, however, is conditional as an organization normally contributes only to parts of a person's total purpose. For example, farmers are perfectly capable of cooperating and do so when necessary; but they do not seek to cooperate in every aspect. What they do is try to manage their social, economic and political problems by forming selective, negotiated alliances (Appadurai 1986, Attwood and Baviskar 1988).

Still, though conditions may be favourable, successful cooperatives are not completely free of conflicts. These, however, largely originate from the outside, but have direct repercussions on the functioning of individual societies. Examples of such potential conflicts are concretely described in

Hedlund (1986). On the one hand, he points at *"state interference"* through an elaborate structure of cooperative legislation and centralized bureaucracy which tend to hamper local initiatives by severely restricting flexibility. This is particularly evident with respect to the financial management of societies, where organizational structure and legislation shifts responsibility and control to higher layers of the cooperative hierarchy.

On the other hand, he points at the potential conflicts embedded in the lack of role fulfilment - as perceived by the members - of a society. From the point of view of the members, an important criterion on society performance is the amount of cash earnings they are able to derive from their membership. In the society studied by Hedlund (1986), fewer conflicts emerged in times of plenty - i.e. periods when the world market prices for coffee were high and the members received substantial incomes. However, when world market prices were depressed and producers felt the pinch of reduced payments, externally imposed export duties, handling charges, cesses, commissions etc., conflicts tended to surface.

The observations above indicate that with the prevailing set up of cooperatives they find themselves in a *"Dependence Trap"* (Figure 2). The point of departure is the role of the government which is responsible for cooperative legislation. This legislation largely predetermines the form and structure of cooperatives, thus infusing a governmental administrative and bureaucratic culture. It is also government legislation that provides the norms for the distribution of loans and subsidies, which frequently leads to an infiltration by political elements and vested interest groups. Additionally, the prevalent culture and norms of institutions such as government departments and financial institutions are not easily changed and often tend to hinder an effective implementation (Paul and Subramaniam 1983:354).

This superstructure imposed by the government, as well as the politicization of societies, tends to sap initiative and motivation and thus have a negative impact. In turn, this will result in poor performance which increases the dependency on the state for additional financial resources. Thus, the cooperatives find themselves locked into a *"vicious circle"*, and it is evident that the prevailing system of cooperation suffers from inherent structural weaknesses.

Co-operatives Reconsidered

The discussion above gives a rather pessimistic view of the possibilities of existing rural development organizational structures to make a positive contribution towards achieving their desired outcomes/goals. An important aspect of the problem is found in the lack of congruence between organizational/superstructure interests and the interest of those served by the organization. This problematique is frequently further exacerbated by State interference into organizational functions at both macro- and micro-levels, and, as a consequence, that local interests are rarely considered (cf. i.a. Hatti and Heimann 1992; Suomela 1991).

Partly, the lack of congruence may indicate a conceptual problem. The terminology used in most of the available literature centres around the concept cooperative(s), thus, indicating a given organizational structure working within a specific legal framework that defines the *limits* for its functioning. Also, by indicating and focusing on the formal cooperative sector, emphasis is placed on an organizational form which - based on experiences of cooperative development in the West, and on how these experiences have been communicated by international donor agencies - basically has been formed in one and the same mould regardless of where in the world a cooperative is found.

In our view, it is necessary to go beyond the formal structures in order to understand the rationality behind an individual's decision to involve himself in cooperative activities or not. To a large extent, as normally used, the very concepts of cooperation and cooperatives carry a moral postulate of rationality, i.e. only by cooperating could higher development objectives be achieved. Also - *"Cooperation is too often seen as a panacea for alleviating poverty in what might be an economically and politically stagnating society."* (Hatti and Heimann 1992:56). It should be borne in mind that cooperation is *not* an aid-giving business (Laidlaw 1978).

More and more evidence has been presented to indicate that cooperation, or cooperative activities, may not be the natural and necessary responses to locally felt development problems. Suomela' (1991:83), for example, talks about an *"identity crisis"* and *"membership alienation"* in many formal cooperative societies during the 1980s.

An important factor generating the situations observed by Soumela concerns the size of cooperative societies. Linked to the question of society size is the fact that a large society must resort to *"indirect forms of democracy"* (Soumela 1991:84). and hence that society decision making may come to represent only the stronger interest group among the members. Additionally, as observed in many cooperative organizations in the Third World, *"...cooperation perhaps might just result in either a redistribution of already scarce resources or aggrandizement of the richer, more powerful participants."* (Hatti and Heimann 1992:56).

Moreover, *"...observations exemplified by such factors as backward bending supply curve of labour must indicate that farmers and peasants in India do not necessarily consider development based on the same economic rational as we,..."* Hatti and Heimann (1992:56). Of particular interest in this context is the discussion on the *"psycho-social value of time"* (ibid.:67). With this concept they want to demonstrate that - although investment and participation decisions cannot be related to an *"economic man"* rationality, frequently presupposed when discussing cooperation and development in Third World contexts - the actual decisions taken may be perfectly rational from the point of view of the individual. In particular, the authors indicate that *"The marginal value of a new labour investment is calculated against the psycho-social value of free time foregone..."* (ibid.). In addition, the importance of free time is that it permits *"...the fulfillment of social obligations and in itself can lead to psychological need-fulfillment."* (ibid.).

Cooperatives have generally not been seen from the point of view of economic rationality. Rather, the focus has been set on the perceived rationality of the work organization through cooperatives. What is frequently forgotten, then, is that cooperatives have to fit into a framework which for the potential members entails not only an economic but also a social reality. In promoting Rural Development, factors such as village social structure, household and family structure, tradition, cultural rules and practices must be considered and incorporated into any plans for rural change.

We argue that cooperation between individuals with common goals of economic self-interest could in many instances be rational, but it has to be developed out of the realization of its benefits to the potential participants. People would accept cooperation if it satisfies some of their significantly felt needs. The concept of an improved quality of life has to be defined by the people themselves. Ultimately only organizations established and promoted by people themselves can initiate and sustain a development process. In this context, a cooperative framework, following the cooperative principles, can have distinct advantages in attaining the objectives of rural development.

Cooperatives, born out of the felt needs of the people, can internalize economic and social development through voluntary action.

This, however, presupposes a reversal of the role of the State in introducing and utilizing cooperative organizations in efforts of rural development - *viz.* State interference has to go from one of a negative influence to one of a positive support (cf. i.a. Gyllström and Rundquist 1989). The rigidity and politicization of existing cooperative structures, as indicated in Figure 2, together with an emphasis on the economic aspects of these organizations is in this context particularly problematic. One aspect of the problematique is the seemingly general decline in respect for authority, including a lack of regard for governmental representatives, civil servants, or politicians as people seem to expect little guidance from them. In addition, governmental policies and bureaucratic (mal)practice are not conducive to cooperation, and do not constitute role models in cooperation and public spirit.

In the course of introducing development programmes based on the principles of cooperation, then, the individuals involved must be convinced that change is possible and can be influenced thorough concerted action. It cannot be taken for granted that the individuals forming the target group for a cooperative project believe that economic and social development is possible and desirable, Moreover, it cannot be taken for granted that they consider cooperation an effective means of achieving their goals and aspirations - at least not if they associate *'cooperation'* with a state controlled organization.

Target groups must perceive an underlying rationality to cooperation, which must be seen as a viable method of achieving collective and individual goals. Cooperation must also be perceived as satisfying in psycho-social terms and not detrimental to psycho-social need fulfilment. Working together in informal constellations towards achieving common goals can lead to a sustainable dynamic that could transcend the task at hand and provide an impetus for concerted development oriented action in general.

A major problem in development policy formulation and programme planning, however, is to create an environment conducive to working together - or, in other words, to cooperation. In our view, such environments are not established as a result of the common way in which development programmes in general, and cooperative projects in particular, are implemented. With respect to the latter, project implementation usually implies the establishment of a full-fledged cooperative structure in terms of organization, linkages and legislation. Once this has been achieved, it is taken for granted that the membership cadre will grow and that cooperation between members will be established. In view of the critical discussion concerning the formal cooperative sector presented above, however, this sector may within itself carry the seeds of failure by alienating potential members from one another, as well as from the very idea of cooperation.

Cooperation is a means for self-help; the idea of working together must come from within the community and be allowed to become habit forming. When and if it is found to be an effective means of achieving personal as well as community goals, cooperation in a more formal sense can emerge from such experiences of informal cooperation. Seen from a planning perspective, the idea of cooperation should be allowed to mature in the course of a *pre-cooperative phase*. During this phase, initially less emphasis should be placed on the formal aspects of cooperation. Instead, it is of paramount importance that potential members are provided with an opportunity to learn to function as a group, since the Indian villagers *"...are more concerned about the mastery of human relationships, than they are about the mastery of things."* (Beals 1974:11). This implies an emphasis on social, rather than purely economic, activities, which eventually could result in a positive group cohesiveness. Once this objective has been achieved, the potential members can be trained in the formal aspects of cooperation.

An important precondition for this concept to be successful is the liberalization of the rigid framework of state policies *vis-à-vis* cooperatives. The role of the state and other implementing agencies, should be to create an environment conducive to cooperation. This presupposes the willingness of the State to allow the concept of 'self-help', both in a social as well as in economic terms to be an integral part of any rural development policy. State policies, thus, must actively change the *'appreciated environment'* of rural development organizations in general and cooperatives in particular.

References

Appadurai A (1986): 'Class, Cooperation and Well Irrigation in Western India.' In Attwood, D.W., Israel, M. and Wagle, N. (eds.) *Dynamics of an Agrarian Society: Maharashtra, India*, University of Toronto Press, Toronto.

Apthorpe R (1972): *Rural cooperatives and planned change in Africa: An analytical overview.* United Nations Research Institute for Social Development - UNRISD, Geneva.

Attwood DW, Baviskar BS (eds.) (1988): *Who Shares? Co-operatives and Rural Development.* Oxford University Press, Dehli.

Beals A (1974): *Village Life in South India; Cultural Design and Environmental Variation.* Chicago University Press.
Bengtsson B (ed.) (1979) *Rural Development Research - the Role of Power Relations.* SAREC REPORT, R4:1979, Swedish Agency For Research Cooperation With Developing Countries.
Chambers R (1974): *Managing Rural Development*, Scandinavian Institute of African Studies, Uppsala.
Chambers R (1983): *Rural Development, Putting the last first.* Longman, London.
Chopra K, Kadekodi GK, Murty MN, (1990): *Participatory Development, People and Common Property Resources.* Sage Publications, New Dehli.
Dantwala ML (1980): 'The Eluding Panacea; the Basic Needs Approach to Indian Planning'. Proceeding and Papers of a Seminar (Trivandrum, July 21-22, 1980. *ILO Asian Employment Programme*, Bangkok.
Dasgupta A (1984): 'Sharing Approaches that Work', *SPAN* Vol. XXV, No.6, June.
Desai DK, Prakash H, (1974): 'Strategy for Rural Development for Weaker Sections', Paper presented to a Seminar on Rural Development,, *Indian Society of Agricultural Economics*, Bombay.
Esman & Uphof (1988): *Local Organizations - Intermediaries in Rural Development.* Cornell University Press, Ithaca and London.
Gohlert EW, (1987): 'Strategic Organizations' - Development Agencies of the Future?. *Scandinavian Journal of Development Alternatives*, Vol. VI No. 4, December, pp. 108-122.
Gyllström B (1989): 'Administered Interdependences vs Spatial Integration' - The Case of Agricultural Service Cooperatives in Kenya. In Gyllström, B. and Rundquist, F-M. (eds.) 1989: *State, Cooperatives and Rural Change.* Lund Studies in Geography, Ser. B. No. 53, Lund.
Gyllström B (1991): *State-Administered Rural Change - Agricultural Cooperatives in Kenya.* Routledge, London.
Gyllström B, Rundquist F-M (eds.) (1989): *State, Cooperatives and Rural Change.* Lund Studies in Geography, Ser. B. No. 53, Lund.
Harriss J (ed.) (1984): *Rural Development; Theories of Peasant Economy and Agrarian Change.* Hutchinson University Library, London.
Hatti N, Heimann J (1992): 'Limits to Cooperation'. *Asian Journal of Economics and Social Studies*, Vol. 11, No. 1, pp. 55-71.
Hatti N, Rundquist F-M (1989a): 'Cooperatives in Rural Development, Land Ownership and Cooperative Membership in Sirsi Taluk, Karnataka State, India'. *MAPALLO*, Vol. 10:3.
Hatti N, Rundquist F-M (1989b): 'Cooperatives in Rural Development in India', Modern Inputs, Production Structure and Stratification in Sirsi Taluk, Karnataka State. In Gyllström and Rundquist (eds.) (1989): *State, Cooperatives and Rural Change.* Lund Studies in Geography, Ser. B. No. 53, Lund.
Hedlund H (1986): *Kaffe, Kooperation och Kultur, En studie av en kooperativ kaffeförening i Kibirigwi, Kenya.* Nordiska Afrikainstitutet, Uppsala.
Hill P (1987): *Development Economics on Trial.* Cambridge University Press, Cambridge.
Holmén H (1991): *Building Organizations for Rural Development, State and Cooperatives in Egypt.* Lund University Press.

Hunter G (1971): 'Lessons from India's Administration of Rural Development'. *Development Digest*, Vol.IX:3.

Hydén G (1980): 'Cooperatives and the Poor': Comparing European and Third World Experience. *Rural Development Review*, Vol. II, No. 1, pp. 9-12.

Hydén G (1983): *No Shortcuts to Progress*. African Development Management in Perspective. Heineman, London.

Jain LC, Krishnamurthy BV, Tripathi PM, (1985): *Grass Without Roots, Rural Development under Government Auspices*. Sage, New Dehli.

Johnston BF, Clark WC, (1982): *Redesigning Rural Development, A Strategic Perspective*. The John Hopkins University Press, Baltimore.

Laidlaw AF (1978): 'Cooperatives and the Poor: A Review from within the Cooperative Movement'. In *Cooperatives and Poor*, London ICA, pp. 51-90.

Lea DAM, Chaudhri DP (eds.) (1983): *Rural Development and The State, Contradictions and Dilemmas in Developing Countries*. Methuen, London.

Lorsch JW, Allen SA (1973): *Managing Diversity and Interdependence*, Harvard University Press, Boston.

Mars T (1986): 'State and Agriculture in Africa': A Case of of Means and Ends. In Developmental States and African Agriculture. *IDS Bulletin*, Vol. 17, No. 1, pp. 16-21.

Mascharenas RC (1988): *A Strategy for Rural Development*, Dairy Cooperatives in India. Sage Publications, New Dehli.

Nair CNS (1981): 'Some Issues in Rural Development Administration', *Indian Management* 20, January 1.

Paul S, Subramaniam A (1983): 'Development Programmes for the Poor; Do Strategies make a difference', *Economic and Political Weekly*, Vol. XVIII, March 5.

Programme Evaluation Organization (1978): 'Evaluation of the working of Antyodaya Programme'. *Planning Commission*, New Dehli.

Rao VM (1983): 'Barriers in Rural Development', *Economic and Political Weekly*, Vol. XVIII, July 2.

Robertson AF (1984): *People and State. An Anthropology of Planned Development*. Cambridge University Press.

Sandbrook R (1985): *The Politics of African Stagnation*. Cambridge University Press.

Smith E, Lethem FJ, Thoolen BA (1980): 'The Design of Organizations for Rural Development Projects' - A Progress Report. *World Bank Staff Working Paper* No. 375.

Srivastava UK et al. (1975): *Planning and Implementation of Rural Development Projects of a Voluntary Agency*, Monograph No.56, Indian Institute of Management, Ahmedabad.

Suomela K (1991): 'The Basic Values of Consumer Cooperation', *The Cooperator*, Vol. XXIX No. 4, August 15, 1991.

Thompson JD (1973): *Hur organisationer fungerar*. Prisma, Stockholm.

Varma RP, Pillai ARR (1980): 'Rural Development: Concept, Process and Problems', *Khadi Gramodog*, October 1.

UNDP (1984): *Rural Cooperatives*. United Nations Development Programe, Mimeographed.

Chapter Four

Why is Local Participation so Weak?

- Twenty-five years of organization building in Muda, Malaysia[1]

By Magnus Jirström

Introduction

The problems of environmental degradation[2] in Third World countries are receiving growing attention from governments, aid organizations and students of Third World development. Most attention has, perhaps, been focused on the consequences of non-sustainable land use in marginal and environmentally fragile areas. Degradation problems are, however, not limited to the less favoured lands. On more favoured lands, characterized by intensive production systems, environmental degradation is often associated with an overexploitation of the traditionally stable agro-ecosystems and/or an introduction of agricultural techniques which disrupt the balance of these systems.

Although the problems of environmental degradation may vary widely, they tend to have features in common as well. One important observation is that efforts aimed at either preventing degradation or halting on-going processes of degradation, often result in failure unless the local people, who use the land/water resource, are playing an active role. The lack of local participation is a problem often referred to in this context. Most existing forms

---

1 Please see page 104 for a brief presentation of the research project that forms the background for the present paper.
2 Examples of important processes of environmental degradation are soil erosion, alkalinisation, salinisation, waterlogging, weed infestation and bush encroachment (Blaikie 1985).

83

of rural organizations, especially those controlled by government agencies, seldom receive support from the grass-roots level of society and are therefore particularly unsuitable for tasks which demand broad communal cooperation.

This paper discusses the absence of locally based farmers' organizations in the Muda Irrigation Scheme in northwest Peninsular Malaysia. In this large-scale Green Revolution area, agro-ecological changes have resulted in serious problems of pests and weed infestations. These problems presently cause instability in yields and constitute an economic threat to the mostly small-scale and resource-poor Muda farmers. For the farmers there is an urgent need to find forms for cooperation in the management of irrigation water and the control of pests and weed infestations. The Farmers' Organizations in Muda have, in spite of being subjects of impressive allocation of government funds for more than two decades, obvious problems in activating farmers in small groups for synchronized farming practices. Why is local participation so weak?

Background

During the past decade development research has increasingly turned attention to the growing number of rural people who somehow must earn their livelihood on a land base that is not expanding. The tendency of governments to favour urban areas and to neglect the rural poor is now well documented. As a reaction to the "urban bias" in Third World development (Lipton 1977, Chambers 1983), the calls for broad-based development have grown in strength. Along with the "discovery" of a need for rural development, an awareness of the importance of rurally based organizations has grown. As agents of change, such organizations can contribute to development. At present this discussion forms part of the broader theme of "institution building" or "institutional development".

Among those concerned with agricultural development in the Third World, the need for locally based farmers' organizations has long been recognized. Traditionally the emphasis has been on creating and/or supporting organizations through which production-oriented services could reach the individual farm household. Examples of organizations which, at various levels, play an active role in agricultural development range from government agencies providing different forms of assistance (agricultural research, extension, credit, marketing service, irrigation facilities, etc.) to so called local organizations (LOs), for example, agricultural cooperatives, farmers' associations, water users' groups and tenant leagues.

Whereas government agencies traditionally have carried out services down to the district level, the intention has often been that activities at the village level should be the responsibility of LOs. On the whole, there seems to be a growing consensus that locally based membership organizations could play an important role as intermediaries between small farmers and government agencies (Esman & Uphoff 1984).

However, experience drawn from studies of the development of agricultural cooperatives in Africa and Asia, clearly points at the negative consequences of efforts trying to create and support such organizations through government involvement and control (Gyllström 1989; Ståhl 1989; Holmén 1989 1991; Hatti & Rundquist 1989; Jirström 1989). The risk of ending up with inefficient, élite-favouring and totally government dependent organizations has, so far, proved to be very high.

Criticism of government involvement in LOs does not necessarily stem from a view of the state as being exploitative, élite-oriented and corrupt in its relation to the poor. It does not deny the necessary role of governments in formulating sound economic policies or in providing infrastructural investments, appropriate technologies, and adequate public services for the rural areas. Criticism of government involvement in LO's simply says that such involvement too often results in weak organizations which, lacking their potential intermediary role, can contribute little to development. The criticism, thus, contests the view, that a major reason for poor performance of cooperatives is a general lack of government funds.

Considering the earlier mentioned "urban bias" in Third World development, it may be tempting to suggest increased government funding, as a cure for weak local organizations. However, government support has often turned out to be a disservice. As I will try to show by using the development of Farmers' Organizations in the Muda Irrigation Scheme in Malaysia as an example, government promotion of organization building at the grass-roots level, may fail in spite of good intentions and massive financial investments. Before turning to this topic, some more general comments on the rural development policy of Malaysia are necessary.

Rural Development Policy in Malaysia

Malaysia is often regarded as a successful example of economic development in the Third World. The country has enjoyed strong growth rates in the past three decades.[3] Since 1957, when independence from British rule was granted, important changes in the structure of the economy have occurred. From being a typical colonial economy heavily dependent on the export of a few raw materials, tin and rubber, the economy of today is not only more diversified but also more urban and industrial-based.

In spite of its rapid urban and industrial growth, Malaysia does not belong to the group of developing countries which for decades could be characterized by their conspicuous urban bias in development efforts. In contrast to some of its regional country neighbours, in particular Thailand, Malaysia has become known for its geographically relatively balanced growth. Partly this can be explained by its success in allocating a relatively large share of foreign investments to the rural areas. More important however, has been the outspoken policy of the ruling government alliance, since 1973 named the National Front (*Barisan Nasional*), to eliminate the division of society into, on the one hand, a modern, progressive, Chinese dominated urban sector and, on the other hand, a predominantly Malay, low-income, traditional rural sector.

This social, economic and geographical division of the multi-ethnic society[4] was inherited from the British. In the 1930's the colonial power had introduced a reservation legislation which prohibited land transfers from Malays - *the bumiputera*[5] - to non-Malays. By doing that, the British gained a number of advantages. The rice sector dominated by small-scale Malay peasants would continue to produce the staple food of the country without being disturbed by Chinese or Indian immigrants who instead could make up

---

3 Real GDP went up by an estimated 6% in the 1960's to 8% per annum in the 1970's (Lim and Muhammad 1989). In the 1980-1985 period GDP growth was 5.5% in 1985-1989 it was 6.2% (UN 1991).

4 In 1970, the ethnic composition of the population of Peninsular Malaysia was 53.2% Malay, 35.4% Chinese, 10.0% Indian and 0.8% others (Watson Andaya & Andaya 1982).

5 After the formation of Malaysia in 1963, the term *bumiputera* "sons of the soil" was created to refer to the indigenous peoples and the Malays (Watson Andaya & Andaya 1982)

the necessary cheap labour for the tin mining industry, the plantation sector and the expanding trade and manufacturing industries in the urban areas. Through the creation of the so called Malay protected lands the Malay community was protected against the economically more assertive non-Malays (Lim 1989). By dividing the non-Malay interest into areas where they would not largely conflict with the *bumiputera* - the British created a balance between ethnic groups but at the same time they created an economy with closed sectors that, in decades to follow, came to show major differences in economic growth.

In 1975, almost two decades after independence, 44% of Malaysian households earned an income below the government set poverty line.[6] 87% of these poor households were in the rural areas. In West Malaysia 74% of the poor were Malays (Daane 1982). In 1970, the average per capita income of Malays was roughly one-half of that of the Chinese (Scott 1985).

Taking into account the above-mentioned facts, it is not surprising that rural development efforts constitute a central part of the, in 1970, enacted *Bumiputera* policy. Thus, the desire to improve the standard of living of the Malays and thereby reduce the potential threat of inter-ethnic conflicts in society, is a central part of the policy. It would, however, be misleading not to point at the nature of political competition since independence. The dominant political party in the coalition is the United Malay Nationalists' Organization (UMNO) - an exclusively Malay Party that depends largely on Malay votes to remain in power (Scott 1985). The vote of the rural Malay population is crucial for the government coalition which has been in power since independence.

As a consequence of the described situation, all but the first out of Malaysia's five national five year plans[7] (1956-1980), have allocated more funds to the rural areas and agricultural development, than to any other sector (Daane 1982). It has been estimated that public expenditure for rural development under the various development plans has ranged between 52.9% and 61.2% of the total non-security development expenditure (*ibid.*). Of the

---

6 The incidence of poverty is far higher among rice farmers than any other major occupational group. In 1975, 77% of the paddy growing households earned incomes below the the poverty line (Daane 1982).

7 The two first plans were the Five Year Plan 1956-1960 and 1961-1965. The three consecutive plans were termed the Malaysia Plans (1966-70, 1971-75, 1976-80) (Daane 1982).

three sub-sectors within the agricultural sector, the estate sector (almost entirely export-oriented), the traditional peasant sector (mainly consisting of rubber small-holders and small-scale rice farmers) and the land settlement schemes, the latter two have clearly received the most attention (*ibid*).

As the main rural development goal was to increase agricultural output and productivity and thereby increase the incomes of rural households, public funds were directed to the construction of infrastructure, the development of high yielding rice varieties and rubber clones, the dissemination of new agricultural technologies through extension activities and to the provision of credit and marketing services and subsidies (fertilizer and price of rice). *Rural development in the case of Malaysia has to a large extent meant agricultural development.*

Although it would be an overstatement to talk of a rural bias in the economic development of Malaysia - one has to consider the importance of the mainly private sector in urban development - it can hardly be disputed that there has been a long-term, conscious effort to channel economic growth so that the rural areas benefit more.

Farmers' Organizations in Muda

The Muda Irrigation Scheme is the nation's largest agricultural development project. It was implemented between 1966 and 1974 and, at present, provides irrigation water for some 50,000 farm families cultivating rice on approximately 100,000 hectares of land in the state of Kedah and Perlis. This region is the traditional "rice-bowl" of Peninsular Malaysia (Figure 1) where farmers, prior to the project were basically subsistence oriented, and had long been among the poorest in Malaysia (Afifuddin 1978). The project is an important example of government investment in rural development. Combining the fact that 97% of the Muda farm households are Malay with the earlier made comments on the electoral interest of government, it is little wonder that rice sometimes has been referred to as a "political crop".

The partly World Bank financed Muda project is administrated by the quasi-governmental agency Muda Agricultural Development Authority (MADA), established in 1970. Thanks to its organizational set-up, MADA enjoys considerable independence in its planning and operation of rural development projects within the Muda area. The agency is responsible directly to the Minister of Agriculture and has in relation to the state level administration an unique autonomy.

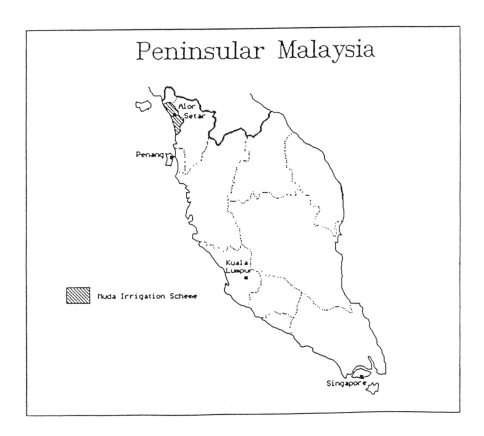

Figure 1: The Muda Irrigation Scheme

For administrative and organizational purposes, the entire Muda Scheme is divided into 27 farm localities. In each of these is sited a *Komplek Geraktani* (Farmers' Movement Complex) supporting approximately 2,000 farm households on approximately 3,000 to 5,000 hectares of rice land. They are geographically determined so that no farmer should have to travel more than 3 miles to reach them. These agricultural development centres each houses the

Farmers' Association (FA), or Farmers' Organization (FO)[8] as well as the office for the irrigation inspectors and irrigation overseers from the Engineering Division of MADA. In importance the FA overshadow all other organizations at the *Komplek Geraktani*. They are the central units in MADA's organizational set-up (Figure 2), responsible for providing services including extension, supply, credit and marketing.

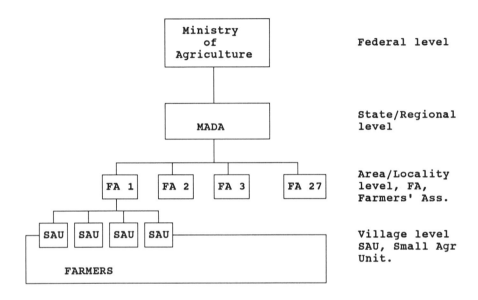

Figure 2: Organizational structure of the Farmers' Association in Muda

This set-up reflects the "Area Development" strategy adopted by MADA. It aims at concentrating resources and efforts in areas having a good infrastructural base and a high potential for sustaining economic growth (Fredericks *et al.* 1980). The strategy was formulated on a national level in the 1960's and was set into practice through the introduction of Farmers'

---

8 The name Farmers' Organization (FO) was introduced in Malaysia in 1973 in order to co-ordinate and integrate the efforts of the Farmers' Associations (FAs) and the remaining agro-based cooperative which since the introduction of FAs had been rivals. In the case of Muda, all the 27 FAs have been registered as Farmers Organizations (FO). In MADA documentation the names used are FA and SAU respectively.

Associations. The formation of FAs had been inspired by the experiences of the Farmers' Association in Taiwan which, successfully, had adopted an integrated development framework.

In the planning of the Muda Scheme, discouraging experiences of the existing agro-based cooperatives in the area, made MADA choose a development approach based on active government involvement in the sub-regional organizations of farmers. The importance of rural development was not only seen in a long-term perspective. The growing political pressure from the rural Malays made rapid rural development programmes like the Muda Scheme a political necessity. At the time, the government did not view the weakness of rural organizations as a problem of too much government involvement but rather the reverse. Government involvement would in the long run be reduced or as declared in the case of MADA:

> "The FA movement aims at motivating farmers to participate in their own organizations actively, so that ultimately, the role of management will be transferred back to the hands of the farmers" (Ho 1980:7).

Thus, in its move to replace one type of government created - but not functioning - grass-root organization with another, MADA stressed its direct influence over the new one. The FA organizational set-up followed the "authority-and-ability-separated system". According to this system, the formulation of policies is to be made by the members' representatives, while management is to be carried out by a technically qualified staff - manager and agricultural technicians - who are appointed by MADA and paid by government. This system was, according to MADA (*Ho 1980*), a way to overcome the problems of a relatively low educational level and lack of organizational ability among the local leaders.

The fundamental units of the FAs are the Small Agricultural Units (SAU) operating at the village level (Figure 2). These should form the link between the ordinary members and the FA. Once in every two years, the SAU elects leaders and representatives to the FA representative assembly which elects the board of directors of the FA. At least once a year, the SAU holds a meeting during which staff members of the FA provide information about the FA activities, while members are given the opportunity to ask questions and to express opinions.

Strength at the Macro-level - Weakness at the Micro-level

Much has been written and said about the general role and performance of the FAs in Muda. Depending on what one wants to measure it is possible to come up with both positive and negative comments on the functioning of the FAs. In his thesis, Afifuddin (1978) points at the importance of the FAs in articulating the interests of the peasants. He refers to the Representative Council of FA Chairmen (*Majlis Perundingan Pergerusi-pergerusi Persatuan Peladang Muda*) introduced in 1975, which constitutes a strong pressure group for the Muda peasantry. Claiming to represent more than 20,000 member-families in the politically important Muda area, the FA, through its Representative Council, can easily catch the attention of both the state and the federal government. The number of generous increases of the price subsidy for rice during the last decade is sometimes referred to as an example of the influence of the FA movement. Thus, the capacity of the FAs to make use of the collective power of farmers at macro-levels, has been put forward as a sign of their overall success.

An attempt to give more comprehensive evaluating comments on the FA performance is not in the scope of this paper. For the purpose of this paper, only the most commonly observed characteristics of the FAs need to be commented on. A general evaluation would, by necessity, have to relate the overall performance of the Muda Irrigation Scheme to the central role that the FAs have played in development. Considering that the Muda scheme, in terms of productivity increases and improvements of farm incomes, has been successful (Jirström 1993a), it would be impossible to deprive the FAs' of their share of that success.

On the other hand, the most serious critique of the Muda Scheme, which is well in line with the mainstream critique of the Green Revolution (*ibid.*), is that the benefits of the agricultural change has reinforced the already unequal pattern of income distribution. In relation to the poor, the rich have become richer. It is from this perspective that much of the critique against the role of the FAs has been leveled. The bulk of the critique of the FAs in Muda can be divided into five categories:

1. The FA is an organization for only a part of the Muda farmers. Although figures of affiliation to the FAs vary in the range of 35-50% depending on sources, the most common estimate referred to, indicates that

approximately 40% of the Muda households are members (Ho 1980, 1985; Daane 1982; Scott 1985).

2. The fact that the majority of Muda farmers are not part of the government-led agricultural organization building, grows in importance when combined with data on membership categories. Several studies show that the FAs are mainly organizations of the relatively well-to-do farmers operating on above average size of land[9] (Fredericks *et al.* 1980, Daane 1982, Scott 1985). In this respect, the Muda FAs follow a pattern all too often observed in studies of rural organizations in the Third World.

3. According to one line of criticism, the FAs have become too dependent on the government agency MADA. The "authority-and-ability-separated system" of FA management, in which MADA appoints and employs the staff has, according to Daane (1982), resulted in a situation where the constituted influence of farmers' representatives in practice is curtailed. The staff, which actually serves two masters, give priority to the interest of MADA as it is their superiors in MADA who determine transfers, promotions and conditions of service. The FAs dependency on MADA can be described by quoting an extract from James C. Scott's book "Weapons of the weak" (1985:126):

> "When farmers speak of the Farmers' Association they call it MADA, referring not to the Farmers' Association or its elected leadership, but to the government agency that directs its activities."

4. The FAs have, according to Scott (1985), also become totally politicized organizations. In his study of a Malay village in Muda, Scott (*ibid.*) observed, that members of the Malay opposition political party (*Partei Islam*, PAS) had never joined the FA because the organization was in the

---

[9] Daane (1982) explains the dominance by relatively bigger-scale farmers by pointing at the fact that small-scale farmers gain little by joining the organization. In his study, "Responses of peasant paddy growers to Farmers' Organizations in West Malaysia", he shows that the strongest incentive for joining the FA is the possibility to receive production credits. For small-scale farmers the cost involved in obtaining FA credit is simply higher than that of the traditional source of production credit, the local, usually Chinese, shopkeeper.

control of the ruling party (UMNO). His conclusion is that the FAs (except for one or two) have become the creature of rich peasants affiliated with UMNO. In Muda and the whole of the state of Kedah, there is a strong competitive situation between the two major Malay-based parties (UMNO and PAS). After the 1978 general election, PAS, in the Muda area, was able to claim to have a majority of Malay votes (although failing to capture the State Government) compared with UMNO (Mansor 1982). Considering the fact that a great number of Muda farmers sympathize with PAS, the politicization of the FAs in favour of the UMNO supporters, significantly reduces the organizations possibility of getting a broader support.

5. The last category of criticism deals with the limited success of the FAs in activating farmers and fostering local cooperation at the village and group levels. At the village level, the Small Agricultural Units (SAUs), which are considered to be *"the fundamental units"* of the FAs (Ho 1985), do not seem to provide a very strong link between the farmers and the FA administration. Limited interest in SAU meetings often result in their canceling due to insufficient quorum (Fredericks *et al.* 1980). In several MADA publications is mentioned the importance of work groups of ordinary peasants which are said to operate at a lower level than the SAUs (Daane 1982). However, in a case study Daane (*ibid.*) found them to be non-existent.

From the above description we can discern a Farmers' Association which, although it for twenty-five years has played a central role in the launching of the Green Revolution in Muda, has not succeeded in one of its major goals - to become an organization run by farmers with the support of a broad participating majority. Although it has succeeded in becoming a politically impressive lobby organization, its politicized role seems to create important drawbacks at the local level. Furthermore, the heavy reliance on government support at all levels has a passivating impact on the farming community. At present, the FAs function mainly as government supported channels to provide services - primarily credit and fertilizers - to the farmers. A central explanation to the fact that the FAs for almost twenty years have not been able to reach a higher membership figure, is that farmers realize that they have little to gain economically by joining.

The important ambition of the FAs - to play an active role in co-ordinating and synchronizing production activities at the farm level - has, on the whole, failed. The provision of farm support services has, with the exception of the efforts to create group-farming projects (see the section on Group Farming in Muda below), been on an individual member basis and reaching only a limited section of the farmers. This fact must be regarded as a major shortcoming in a large-scale irrigation scheme dependent on close cooperation between farmers. During the last decade of increasing problems with shortage of irrigation water and growing problems of insect pests, diseases, and weed infestations, the need for well functioning cooperation at the farm level has become greater than ever.

Environmental Change and the Need for Synchronized Farming

During the first ten years of operation of the Muda Project, 1970-1980, production increased dramatically and the project was, in terms of productivity improvements, often referred to as a Green Revolution success story. Unfortunately, development after 1980 has been less encouraging, showing a pattern of growing instability in production. This instability has partly been due to problems of water shortage (Jirström 1992) and partly to problems of pest and disease outbreaks and weed infestations.

The increasing problems of insect pests, diseases and weed infestations are directly connected to the changes of the physical farm environment that has taken place since the intensification of production in 1970. In the case of insect pests and diseases, the increased cropping intensity and denser planting has resulted in an ideal carry-over system. Furthermore, the traditional periods of fallow during the dry months having dampening effects on pest populations have, through the introduction of year-round water supply, been replaced with a continuous and overlapping plantation of new varieties more susceptible to pests. In addition, the increasing application of nitrogen fertilizers has led to a decrease in natural resistance by making rice much more attractive to many insect pests and diseases (Norton & Way 1990).

In the case of weed infestations, it is the shift in crop establishment method from transplanted to direct seeded rice culture, that explains most of the growing problems (Jirström 1994). This shift has been caused by labour shortage and spiralling labour costs and has occurred during the 1980's. At present the vast majority of farmers are direct seeding. Under this method, the seeds are sown directly in the wet or dry soil of the fields. In contrast to the traditional technique of hand-transplanting seedlings into standing water, the rice plants grown under direct seeding suffer serious competition from weeds which can germinate and grow side by side with the rice plant.

For the individual farmer, the above described problems are difficult to overcome unless he is operating in an environment of close field-neighbour cooperation. As pointed out by Wong (1979:x):

> "...group efforts are seen to be more effective in maintaining the ecological balance of the village environment through minimizing the negative externalities often created when farmers operate independently in pursuit of their own individual goals".

In the Muda context, there are several reasons for the increasing need of close cooperation at the farm level. Some examples will be given below:

1. In the case of weed control under direct seeded conditions, the single most important factor is that of good water management. By gradually introducing water into the field as the plant grows, weeds can be depressed as they do not receive sufficient light. Sufficient water is also important for the success of early herbicide application. Problems in water control normally result in heavy weed infestations reducing yields significantly (*ibid.*). Hence, the relatively newly adopted method of direct seeding, places greater emphasis on well-functioning cooperation in water management. Unsynchronized planting is a common problem making water control difficult. During field work in the area conducted by the author in 1992-93, it was possible to observe several cases where fields neighbouring each other showed a three months difference in harvesting date. This observation was also confirmed by a survey based on agricultural diaries kept by farmers during a period of ten months.

2. Unsynchronized planting reduces the chances of following the MADA recommendation of one yearly month of fallow period over the whole Muda area. This principle was introduced as a measure to control the serious outbreaks of the *Tungro* virus disease in the early 1980's. Introduced in 1984, this measure, by interrupting continuous planting, not only reduced the problems of the virus but also that of the most important

insect pest, the *Brown Plant Hopper* (BPH). In an area where there always are green fields for pests and diseases to thrive, the possibilities of efficient control are reduced.

3. Insect pests, diseases and weeds spread from field to field. For example, wind, water and even tractors and combine harvesters spread seeds of weeds from one field to another. Thus, it is not sufficient for an individual farmer to control his field/fields if there are problems of pests and weeds in the area where he is operating. Therefore, it is essential to keep a whole farm neighbourhood as free as possible of pests and weed infestations. This can only be done if all farmers cooperate. As expressed by one farmer complaining about weed problems:

> "What is the point in struggling to keep my fields clean when some of my neighbours' fields are full of weeds?"

The Response of MADA - Integrated Pest Management

The response of the authority MADA to the growing problems of pests and weeds has been to adopt and pursue the approach of Integrated Pest Management (IPM) which stresses the need of combining different protective measures - manual, mechanical and chemical. The problems of spreading the ideas of IPM to the Muda farmers have been substantial. In contrast to other components of modern agriculture like mechanization, irrigation, chemical fertilizers and standardized agricultural credit, the demands of IPM are less easily understood by small-scale Third World farmers as Goodell (1984:1) points out:

> "...it /IPM/ requires the farmer to grasp a far more complex set of data, data which are often anything but self-evident, unitary and standardized, or amenable to trial-and-error learning."

In her article, Goodell (*ibid.*) brings forward a number of problems in making IPM functional for small-scale farmers in the Third World. Two of them are of immediate interest in the case of Muda. Firstly, she points at something already touched upon in the previous section, namely, that of IPM demanding tighter field-level organization for synchronized planting. Secondly, she warns about the risk of farmers becoming over-dependent on government pest control actions and support. In Muda the authorities provide, free of charge, large-scale pesticide application in serious cases of attack. As Goodell correctly points out, such a policy may have a strongly passivating effect on farmers' attitude to pest problems.

Both these problems have been recognized by MADA. The urgent need for field-neighbourhood based cooperation has become a strong pressure in the on-going Group Farming Project aiming at forming group farming (*Kelompok Tani*) in Muda. Before turning to the development of farming groups, a brief analysis of the difficulties in creating local cooperation will be presented.

Why is Local Participation so weak?

The problem of creating a network of small-scale organizations in the Muda area was realized at an early stage of the development programme. Several explanations for the difficulties in creating broad local participation have been brought forward. Afiffudin (1978) discusses the patterns of settlement in the Muda area. According to his line of reasoning, the fact that most villages in the area are linear settlements and not clustered, explains why neighbourhood or community consciousness is hard to observe. In large parts of Muda, the linear settlement pattern straddles the canals, drains and roads for miles and miles. As experienced by anyone who has tried to identify a village (*kampung*) boundary in Muda, farmers sometimes do not even refer to their residential area as a village, but simply mention the number and section of the drain or canal. Thus, Muda farmers are basically residing in a "canal-based society" and not in a "village-based society" (Affifudin 1977, Ho 1980).

Daane (1982) notes that Muda villages lack the necessary characteristics for being described as social units. The villages have no corporate structure and lack corporate groups above the household level. Instead, social organization is based on dyadic relationships between individuals and households, i.e. *"on ego-focused networks which do not stop at the physical boundaries of the village"* (Daane 1982:72).

After a thorough description of the structural characteristics of two Malay villages, of which one is situated in the Muda area, Daane (*ibid.*) concludes that they appear to be typical of Southeast Asian rice growing villages on plains.[10] Such village societies have also been characterized as *"less institutionalized"* or *"loosely structured"* villages. In villages as these, cooperation aimed at achieving collective goals poses problems. Considering the increasing need for cooperation in farming activities, all of the sociological findings referred to here are of great interest.

Of great interest is, however, also Daane's brief discussion on the influence of government support on the member contribution to the FA-movement. Strong government involvement in *"loosely structured societies"* seems to have important negative consequences. Daane refers to Goodell who points out that lack of corporate action and *"almost pathetic dependence [of peasants on government agencies] and paternalism [of the government] are hallmarks of loose structuration"* (ibid.).

A fact which seems to have further complicated the creation/emergence of broad based local cooperation, is that the farm land which surrounds a village, to a relatively large extent,[11] is cultivated by farmers not residing in the village. This is mainly due to a high degree of mobility and to the pattern of land inheritance.

As has been laid out in this section, farmers tend to be individually oriented and mostly not inclined to engage in long-term group activities. However, these findings contradict the commonly referred to existence of a spirit of mutual help among rural people (*gotong royong*) in Malaysia and Indonesia. The positive references to this spirit is, however, mostly found in official documents recommending rural development projects to make use of the advantageous conditions just waiting to be utilized. Although *gotong*

---

10 The characteristics of such villages are according to Daane (1982:82): "(1) The absence of clear boundaries of the social system, and the absence of a village identity and self-governing organizations; (2) The absence of formal institutions for social control, the weakness of social sanctions and a lack of ability to settle internal disputes; (3) The openness of the village to outsiders who want to move into the village; (4) The reliance of the individual on non-group organizations (e.g. dyads, networks, and chains of alliances), which implies no lasting relationships, the absence of enduring social groups above the household level".

11 In the case study of five Muda villages, the author observed that approximately 30-40% of the fields neighbouring a village were cultivated by farmers not residing in the village (Jirström 1994). Morooka et al. (1991) also point at the problems of coordinating cooperation due to the spread of land cultivated.

royong activities can be observed in Muda villages, their importance should not be romanticized. Again Daane's comment, seems to be relevant (Daane 1982:31):

> "The concept of *gotong royong* as a voluntary free labour service is very much a thing of the past. Villagers now expect payment for their labour contributions to projects at village level that are wholly or partly financed from government funds, such as the building of a bridge and a road."

For the purpose of cooperation in agricultural activities, the concept of *gotong royong* also has clear limitations. The principles of *gotong royong* stresses its voluntary character, something which is reflected by the absence of sanctions against non-fulfillment of *gotong royong* activities. Therefore *gotong royong* is not a good solution to problems which require the participation of all those affected. In, for example, pest and weed control and the coordination of water control and planting schedules, the non-cooperation of only one or a few of the farmers involved could make the entire effort useless. This is a problem often referred to by farmers when cooperation difficulties are discussed.

Group Farming - The Government Plans do not Catch On

The fact that in the Muda area, rice fields in an area often are operated by farmers not residing in the same village has, of course, limited the potential efficiency of the community-based SAU, Small Agricultural Units. In the late 1970's, MADA initiated a Group Farming Project (*Projek Berkelompok*) with the purpose of encouraging member farmers to realize the importance of pooling their efforts and resources into integrated groups (Syed Ahmad and Ho 1985). Thus, in the Muda case, group farming (*Kelompok Tani*) is based on field neighbourhood.

The interest for group farming is, however, not unique for MADA. In most Southeast Asian countries, on-going efforts are being made to establish and possibly institutionalize group farming (Yasunobu *et al.* 1990). Originally, these groups were organized as units of minimum access at the farm level for diffusing improved techniques to rice farmers via the the extension system (Morooka *et al.* 1991). During the last decade, their role and function seem to have been re-evaluated. In several Southeast Asian countries, the traditional basis of rice farming - the family farm being highly dependent on hired and exchange labour - is undergoing change. In certain rural areas experiencing a fast increase in the cost of labour,[12] traditional farm practices involving manpower or draft animals have gradually been replaced by labour-saving technology (*ibid.*). The new technology, for example, mechanical harvesting on contract basis and/or direct seeding, places new demands on the coordination of farm activities and thus on the cooperation between farmers. Through group farming, it is thought, farmers can better negotiate with contractors to set proper fees for land preparation and harvesting. They can also agree on planting schedules and irrigation schedules. In addition to this, the need for improved in-field cooperation in order to limit the problems of pest and weed damage has been increasingly recognized during the 1980's.

Apart from the practical and technical motives for group farming, some more general motives should be mentioned. In Malaysia, the National Agricultural Policy (NAP) relies very heavily on group farming to bring about large increases in production efficiency among smallholders not only in the rice sector, but also in other crops such as rubber, oil palm, cocoa, sugar, fruit and vegetables (Abdul Aziz 1988). In the case of rice, the concept of group farming is also related to the unique government strategy of shifting from rice production by small farmers to that of the estate form (Morooka *et al.* 1991). The estatization strategy was basically a countermeasure against the increasing tendency of land abandonment caused by the outflow of labour to the non-agricultural sectors. Rice estates were to collect land where farmers had given up cultivation. In the case of Muda, the problems of idle land have been negligible. The government strategy of estatization is instead met through the continued efforts of forming group farming projects. Under the group farming project, a certain area of rice fields are managed under the guidance of a few staff members. In that sense they can be said to reflect at least parts of the estatization concept. Furthermore, a number of so called mini-estates (*Separa Perladang*, also referred to as semi-estates) have been formed. The mini-estate could be described as a more advanced form of group farming selected from the more successful group farming projects. A total shift from the concept of group farming to the government strategy of estatization seems less likely due

---

[12] The high pace of economic growth and changes in industrial structure in several Southeast Asian countries, has resulted in rural-urban migration, paticularly of youth, which, in turn, has led to an increased rural wage rates.

to the resistance from farmers who do not own land and thus may be omitted from the group.

After some fifteen years of promotion and support from MADA, the development of group farming has not met with the expected success. As of 1990, some 327 group farming projects (including 51 mini-estates) were registered. However, the majority were not actively managed (Morooka *et al.* 1991). Assuming an average membership of 30 in each group farming project[13] and a total of 130 actively managed projects, the number of Muda farmers involved in functioning group farming would stop below 4,000. This figure, although very approximate, can be compared with the total number of Muda farmers - approximately 50,000. Considering the plans to increase the number of group farming projects to 1,602, including 186 mini-estates, by 1995 (*ibid.*), the authorities seem to have a giant task ahead of them.

Critical voices against the heavy reliance on the group farming concept have been raised. In an article on agricultural development in Malaysia, Abdul Aziz (1988) points out that an important issue is whether civil servants are likely to be successful in significantly improving the management of groups of smallholdings. He also comments (1988:13):

> "The concept of the group management of smallholding has existed in Malaysia since the 1970's. A very small number of cases have been reported, including one in rubber and another in padi [rice], where the smallholders were said to be better off. In each case the conditions were quite exceptional, rather than typical, and there appeared to have been a subsidy element present in each instance."

In the case of Muda, the relatively slow development of group farming cannot be explained by referring to an inability of Muda farmers to adopt new ideas. On the contrary, Muda farmers have, for more than two decades, shown their ability to adapt to a changing farm environment, for example, tractorization, irrigation and double cropping, mechanized harvesting, direct seeding, etc. In order to understand the rather cool interest that farmers have shown for the group farming concept, we have to focus on more tangible reasons such as those discussed previously (pp.11-13). The incongruity of farmers' residence

---

13 In a 1989 study of 10 group farming projects (*Kelompok Tanis*) at the D locality in the District II of the Muda Area, the number of members ranged from 9 to 48, with an average of 28 (Yasunobu *et al.* 1990)

and farming land poses serious problems. To gather farmers for meetings is difficult when they are spread over a vast area. Furthermore, farmers who operate a relatively smaller part of the defined group farming area may be less inclined to participate than those who cultivate a bigger share. Farmers who operate along the canals may feel less dependent on tight cooperation than those in the middle of an irrigation block. Those who only operate on a temporary basis - renting for one season or cultivating only every two or three seasons as a result of the traditional land inheritance system - may also be less interested. Farmers who have important non-farming incomes may be less interested, and so forth.

To these problems should then be added the socio-political problems discussed earlier. Supporters of the opposition party may view the group farming project as a new government party based institution benefiting their political opponents.

Thus, the formation of group farming projects is not an easy task. The concept itself does not work as a cure-all to the problems affecting cooperation between farmers. No matter how well justified the establishment of group farming projects may seem to be, its success will be dependent on the ability to overcome several problems. A condition for success seems to be that they can function in an area with a high degree of land fragmentation.

Concluding Remarks

In this discussion on organization building in the Muda Irrigation Scheme, problems of insufficient cooperation at the farm level have repeatedly been referred to. This emphasis does not stem from findings or experiences showing a general lack of cooperation between farmers in Muda. Of course Muda farmers cooperate in many ways. The problem, however, seems to be that the need for a very tight field cooperation is increasing as new agricultural practices are introduced. For example, new techniques for crop establishment (direct seeding) and harvesting (renting in combine harvesters) place higher demands on coordination and synchronization of farming activities. In the same way, successful control of pests and weeds need more refined forms of cooperation between farmers as well as between farmers and extension staff.

In its urge to introduce new institutional forms for on-farm cooperation, the authorities have launched a Group Farming Project. Inspired, perhaps, by the impressive ability of Muda farmers to adopt to new technology, the planning and implementing authority hopes that the group farming concept will provide the necessary basis for improved cooperation. It needs to be emphasized, however, that the expectation on what group farming can achieve, in the short run, should not be set to high. In a comparison between East Asian and Southeast Asian experiences of local participation in irrigation development, Hayami and Ruttan (1985) refer to the difference in cultural endowments and communal institutions. In the case of, for example, Japan, *"an intensive network of small-scale irrigation systems was build and maintained mainly by communal efforts since the feudal period"*. Leadership, and willingness to support it, developed gradually over generations in response to gradual population pressure on available land. Farmers' participation in group activities has for generations been vital for the survival of their community (*ibid.*).

Unlike the case in East Asia, most parts of Southeast Asia have, until recently, been characterized by an abundant supply of unused land, so that the increasing population could easily be supported by opening new land for cultivation. Although these conditions are changing rapidly, *"the social system molded under the land-abundant conditions does not change so quickly"* (*ibid.*). The authors conclude (*ibid*: 323):

> "Compared with Japan, the social structure in Southeast Asia has remained loose, making it easier to avoid than to participate in group activities."

The Hayami and Ruttan conclusions may, in a discussion of locally based organizations in Muda, remind us of the need to allow institution building to take its time and, furthermore, not to expect, for example, group farming projects to solve too comprehensive tasks in too short a time. Perhaps we can also conclude that the involvement of authorities must be balanced so that it stimulates farmers' participation without strangling it.

The present paper forms a part of the research project "Land Use Intensification - Social and Ecological Impacts". In the study of five selected Muda villages, measurements of weed infestations are being related to the social and economic conditions of farm households. Differences in production and protection activities among households are being related to activities taking part on the village and regional level in order to explain intra- and inter-village differences in levels of weed infestations.

References

Abdul Aziz AR (1988): Agricultural Development in Malaysia: Current Issues and Prospects. *MIER Discussion Paper*, No. 19. Malaysian Institute of Economic Research

Afifuddin O (1978): *Peasants, institutions, and development in Malaysia: The political economy of development in the Muda region*. Ph.D thesis, Cornell University.

Blaikie P (1985):*The Political Economy of Soil Erosion in Developing Countries*. Longman, London & New York.

Chambers R (1983): *Rural Development - Putting the Last First*. Longman, London.

Daane JRV (1982): *Responses of Peasant Paddy Growers to Farmers' Organizations in West Malaysia*. Ph.D thesis, Agricultural University of Wageningen.

Esman MJ, Uphoff NT (1988): *Local Organizations - Intermediaries in Rural Development*. Cornell University Press.

Fredericks LJ, Kalshoven G, Daane JRV (1980): *The Role of Farmers'Organizations in Two Paddy Farming Areas in West Malaysia*. Bulletin No. 40., Afdelingen voor sociale wetenschappen aan de Landbouwhogeschool, Wageningen.

Goodell G (1984): Challenges to International Pest Management Research and Extension in the Third World: Do We Really Want IPM to Work?. *Bulletin of Entomological Society of America*. 1984, 30. pp18-26.

Gyllström B (1989): Administered Interdependences vs Spatial Integration. The Case of Agricultural Service Cooperatives in Kenya. In Gyllström and Rundquist (Eds.) 1989. pp5-56

Gyllström B, Rundquist FM (Eds.) (1989): *State Cooperatives and Rural Change,* Lund Studies in Geography, Ser. B. Human Geography. 53. Lund University Press.

Hatti N, Rundquist FM (1989): Coopertives in Rural Development in India. Modern Inputs, Production Structure and Stratification in Sirsi Taluk, Karnataka State. In Gyllström B. and Rundquist F.M. (Eds.) 1989. pp130-149.

Hayami Y, Ruttan V (1985): *Agricultural Development: An International Perspective*. The Johns Hopkins University Press, London.

Ho NK (1980): *The Framework of Agricultural Extension Programme in the Muda Scheme: A Quick Glimpse.* Monograph No. 39. MADA, Muda Agricultural Development Authority, Alor Setar

Holmén H (1989): State, Cooperatives and Development: Egypt 1908-1988. In Gyllström and Rundquist (Eds.) 1989. pp90-129.

Holmén H (1991): *Building Organization for Rural Development - State and Cooperatives in Egypt.* Lund University Press, Lund.

Jirström M (1989): *Agricultural Cooperative in Zimbabwe.* Rapporter och Notiser Nr. 90, Department of Social and Economic Geography, Lund University.

Jirström M (1992): Förändrade krav på vattenförsörjningen i Muda, Malaysia. *Geografiska Notiser* 1992:1. pp4-12.

Jirström M (1993a): Intensive Rice Cultivation - Problems of Pests and Diseases, A Case Study of the Muda Irrigation Scheme, Malaysia. In Dahl J, Drakakis-Smith D, Närman A (Eds.) *Land, Food and Basic Needs in Developing Countries.* Publications Ser. B, Nr. 83. Departments of Geography, University of Göteborg. pp 77-101.

Jirström M (1994): Weed and Wealth in Muda - Capital intensive weed management - a growing problem for resource-poor farmers in Muda, Malaysia. Forthcoming in *Kajian Malaysia - Journal of Malaysian Studies.* December 1994.

Lim TG (1989): Reconstituting the Peasantry: Changes in Landholding Structure in the Muda Irrigation Scheme. In Hart G, Turton A, White B (Eeds.) *Agrarian Transformations - Local Processes and the State in Southeast Asia.* University of California Press. pp193-212.

Lipton M (1977): *Why Poor People Stay Poor: Urban Bias in World Development.* Harvard University Press.

Mansor O (1982): Political Power and Wealth in the Rural Areas. In *Akademika* No. 20 & 21, 1982. pp373-394.

Morooka Y, Ohnishi A, Yasunobu K (1991): Reciprocal Form of Family Farm and Group Farming - A Perspective of Kelompok Tani in Malaysia and Indonesia. In *Japanese Journal of Farm Management.* Vol. 29, No. 3.

Norton GA, Way MJ (1990): Rice pest management systems - past and future. In Grayson BT *et al.* (Eds.) *Pest Management in Rice.* Elsevier, New York. pp 1-14.

Scott JC (1985): *Weapons of the Weak - Everyday Forms of Peasant Resistance.* Yale University Press.

Ståhl M (1989): Capturing the Peasants Through Cooperatives - The case of Ethiopia. In Gyllström and Rundquist (Eds.) 1989. pp 57-89.

Syed Ahmad A, Ho NK (1985): *Participation of Farmers in the Planning and Implementation of Rural Development Projects: A Case study of the Muda Irrigation Project.* Monograph No. 41, MADA, Muda Agricultural Development Authority, Alor Setar.

UN (1991): *National Accounts Statistics. Analysis of Main Aggregates, 1988-1989.* New York.

Watson Andaya B, Andaya LY (1982): *A History of Malaysia.* Macmillan, London.

Wong J (Ed) (1979): *Group Farming in Asia. Experiences and Potentials.* Singapore university Press.

Yasunobu K, Morooka Y, Wong HS (1990): *Kelompok Tani and Communal Ties among Rice Farmers in the Muda Area, West Malaysia.* Report prepared for the Quarterly Meeting on the MADA/TARC Joint Research Programme June 1990.

Chapter Five

Agro-industries, Cooperatives and Rural Development in the Philippines

By Esteban N. Pagaran

Introduction

The role of agro-industries[1] in promoting rural development has been the subject of divergent views. The "Food First" school of thought, exemplified by the writings of Lappe and Collins (1977) argued that agro-industries hurt small farmers by exposing them unfairly to efficient competitors that have formidable financial and technical resources at their disposal. Moreover, agro-industries tend to encourage small farmers to shift their production out of the traditional food crops and to cause a decline of their nutritional standards. This view was criticized by Glover (1990) for lack of empirical evidence and reliance on journalistic sources of information

The other school of thought (Goldberg 1979; Austin 1983; Goldsmith 1985) believes that agro-industries can help small farmers and develop rural areas in the Less Developed Countries (LDC). This school argues that small farmers would benefit through access to credit, technology, and the market. A recent comparative study (Valdes 1991) of small farmers engaged in export crop production in Asia, Africa and Latin America seems to confirm this view. Contrary to the common belief that cultivating cash crops exposes them to risk of food scarcity and nutritional deficiency, the study revealed that farmers

---

1 "An Agro-industry is an enterprise that processes agricultural raw materials, including ground and tree crops as well as livestock. It is essentially processing and thus represents only one component of the larger, seed-to-consumer agribusiness system. The degree of processing can vary tremendously ranging from cleaning and grading of apples to the milling of rice, to cooking, mixing, and chemical alteration that create a textured vegetable food" (Austin,1981, p. 3).

would attempt to balance the expansion of cash crop production with food needs. Small farmers who shifted cultivation into sugar cane, maize, vegetables and rice for export either maintained or marginally improved the nutrition levels of their families while raising their incomes. This research further revealed that farmers continue to produce subsistence crops as a risk-aversion measure against market and production risks. Their concern for food security, the study deduced, created the incentive to adopt modern technology for staple food production to cope with the demand for expanded production in cash cropping. The study concluded that the switch to production for export increased the demand for hired labor and therefore generated increased employment.

A more comprehensive view considers agro-industries as an element of a rural development strategy that is envisaged to generate distinct benefits. First, agro-industries are expected to reduce migration to cities as industries are brought to the countryside. This in effect would ease pressure or demand for urban infrastructure, housing and other amenities. Secondly, the retention of labor in the rural areas would have the beneficial effect of reducing prices for commodities since wage costs are cheaper in rural areas. Thirdly, agro-industries could prevent "skill drain" from rural areas if industrial activities in the countryside provide reasonable opportunity for employment for the well-educated rural residents either as a worker or owner-manager. Fourthly, from a broader perspective, agro-industry could lead to regional equity and provide developmental spinoff through deepening of rural skills (Saith 1991). The experience of Taiwan is cited to support this view. The development of diversified agro-industries contributed significantly to rural development and decentralized industrialization in that country (ibid., 1991;Ho, 1979).

Most writings on the role of agro-industries in rural development have been rather negative. White's (1983) study of the effectiveness of agro-industries in promoting rural development in Ghana revealed that they failed because projects were chosen without consulting local population. Local participation was ignored and indigenous agricultural tradition was disregarded. Furthermore, location evaluation was inappropriate with sources of raw material remotely situated.

The negative impacts of agro-industry in traditional rural life have been addressed in several studies. Pantasen's study of agro-industries in Thailand (1989) found that farmers depended on the agro-industry for the supply of capital, technology and marketing. The production system resulted in mono-cropping because the agro-industries dictated what crop the farmers should plant. Moreover, mono-cropping also enhanced farmers' vulnerability to the uncertainties of weather, pests and price fluctuations.[2] The author also feared the uprooting of local knowledge of the cultivation of traditional crops.

Santika's study (1990) of Indonesian experience revealed that certain sectors of the agro-industries are suitable to generate employment while others are not. In general, Glover (1990) suggests that the success or failure of agro-industries to achieve rural development objectives is contingent on the specific circumstances and arrangements under which they operate. The location, institutional arrangement and the type of crops grown determine these conditions.

Stanford's inquiry (1989) into Mexican agro-industry engaged in cantaloupe production showed that the relations between the agribusiness companies and contract growing farmers' association was neither smooth nor beneficial to the small farmers. Antagonism characterized the relationship between the small farmers and the agribusiness companies. The agribusiness companies' control of the price placed the small farmers in a disadvantageous position. In order to lower the prices paid to producers, the agribusiness companies resorted to various practices including raising quality standards and then buying from secondary markets those "rejects" at give-away prices. The conclusion was that cantaloupe production benefitted the agribusiness companies but not the small farmers. However, one may wonder why the "rational" peasants did not plant something else if the system was so disadvantageous to them.

A related study (Glover & Klusterer, 1990) comparing agro-industry in Canada and Central America showed that the foremost disadvantage to the small outgrower was the unequal market relation, characterized by virtually only one buyer (monopsony). Nevertheless, agro-industries did improve farmers' income, technological development and regional economic development.

Another positive view of agro-industries' developmental role is given by Goldsmith (1985) who wrote a critical essay about agro-industries based on "case studies" in different parts of the developing world. His study showed that in ten out of twelve cases reviewed farmers did receive higher incomes

---

2 The problem with monoculture is that if one crop fails the farmer is completely ruined for that particular season. Unlike when one has several crops if one crop fails other crops will be available to survive on. Moreover, monoculture is partly blamed for pest infestation. In the case of NFC, this threat is being experienced by the farmers.

because of their linkage with the agro-industry. They benefitted from introduction of new technologies which generated higher productivity. The author underscored the Third World's built-in advantage in developing agro-industries as the technology used is often cheap, small-scale and available within many LDCs.

In one study about an agro-industry in the Philippines Ignacio (1990) focused mainly on agro-industrie's internal corporate and management systems. The study examined the relationship of the agro-industry with different production organizations, namely the contract-grower, the corporate farm and the cooperative.

Under the contract grower system, each farmer signed an agreement to grow a specific crop for the company. The agreement obliged farmers to allocate part of their land to the specified crop, and to sell all their contracted crops to the company. Furthermore, they provide maintenance labor in the farms. During harvest, they pack the crops in preparation for transport to the processing plant. The company for its part furnished the inputs, guaranteed minimum purchase price and provided various forms of cash support for land preparation.

Under the corporate farm scheme, the company rented land from the farmers for a six-month period. During the planting season, wage laborers were hired to cultivate the land. Farmers renting out the land have no further obligation except to make the land available on the specified date for tomato planting. The purpose of limiting the lease period to only six months was to allow the owner-farmers to plant their land with rice during the normal rice-growing season. In addition, this system of intercropping also reduced pest problems.

The cooperative growing scheme was a production contract between the cooperative and the agro-industry firm. The latter provided technical advice and a guaranteed market at a mutually agreed selling price of tomato. Unlike the other schemes mentioned, farmers sourced their funds from private banks. However, the loan was guaranteed by the agro-industry firm and the government's Medium and Small-scale Industry Guarantee Fund.

Ignacio concluded that the cooperative growing scheme was the most advantageous to the farmers. Based on the agreed purchase price and the average productivity of the cooperative farmers, the study inferred that farmers would earn more per hectare than in the other two schemes mentioned.

This conclusion could, however, be challenged on several grounds. Its analysis was confined to financial reports provided by the corporation. The author did not interview farmers to elicit their views on the issue. Under this arrangement, the farmers assume greater financial costs and risks. The study overlooked the effects (whether positive or negative) on the community or region. In retrospect, the assumed productivity level for cooperatives used in the financial estimate of benefits for cooperative contract growing was unusually high for that particular year and it has not been duplicated in the succeeding years. Ignacio also neglected to examine the effect of tenancy on profitability.

Aim and Scope of the Study

The objective of this paper on agro-industries in the Philippines is manifold. Based on empirical data collected from field research in 1991-1992, it analyzes gains and losses accruing to both agro-enterprises and rural households. The analysis sheds light on advantages and disadvantages of agro-industries and on their suitability for the promotion of rural development. The essay also discusses whether agro-industries improve rural incomes, generate employment, and contributes to technology transfer and better local resource management. A central issue is whether organizational form - cooperative, private enterprise or government-owned enterprise - matters for the success of agro-industries.

Before presenting the case-study on organizational form, a brief background will be given, including general information about agro-industries in the Philippines. Also, a short section will present the historical experience of various forms of co-operatives in the country.

Agro-industries in the Philippines

The importance of agro-industries in the Philippine economy has been growing in the past few years. The gross value added of agro-industries is quite substantial compared with other sectors of the economy as the table below shows:

Table 1: Manufacturing

Year	Agro-industries	Other Manufactures [a]
	(in million pesos, at current prices)	
1986	84,938	69,981
1987	96,640	76,861
1988	125,676	81,560
1989	139,444	93,748
1990	158,635	112,771

Source: Philippine Agribusiness Factbook, Center for Resarch and Communication, 1991.
a) The exchange rate is 1 USD = 27 Philippine Peso (PPH)

Despite the growing importance of the agro-industries to the economy there has been a dearth of studies on the subject. The research on the issue is restricted to feasibility studies of individual firms or industry sector studies. One broader study (Hayami *et.al.* 1990) which dealt with the subject concentrated on the socioeconomic context and on the agro-industries' impact on agrarian structure instead of rural development *per se.*

The impetus to develop agro-industries in the Philippines could be traced to several factors. One is that land resources are stagnant as the land frontier was reached in the 1960s (Ofreneo, 1981). At the same time, population continues to grow at a rapid rate of 2.4% annually (Philippine Development Report, 1990) or a population increment of one million annually. One obvious consequence of the failure to generate employment in agriculture while land remains constant was the increasing number of landless in the rural areas (Hayami, 1978).

Another catalyst is government policy. In the mid-1970s, an ILO study (ILO, 1975) showed a lack of rural employment opportunities, widening regional inequality and capital intensive industries. The study recommended that regional policy should be adopted to block this trend and to create livelihood opportunities in the rural areas.

The Philippine government's response to the policy recommendation was to begin a comprehensive credit and advisory program for potential entrepreneurs to develop small and medium-sized agro-industries in rural areas. In addition, banks were required by law to allocate 20% of their loanable funds for financing small and medium-sized industries in these areas.

The government has similarly undertaken livelihood programs for the rural poor that were organized along cooperative schemes. Cooperative organizations were formed by the new land reform beneficiaries. They established their small processing industries where the produce of the land was processed before being sold to the market. More recently, a preferential lending rate policy was established for cooperatives.

The policy of agro-industrialization was further elaborated in the so-called Countryside Agro-industrial Development Strategy. The program aims to promote productivity and modernization of rural industries. In addition, industrial estates for small and medium scale industries were established (Philippine Development Report, 1990).

This initiative was not confined to government institutions alone. The private business sector and non-government organizations (NGOs) established similar programs. The private agribusiness sector has established subcontracting schemes for rural households, entrepreneurs, and cooperative organizations. The NGOs, particularly the cooperative organizations and voluntary welfare associations, were active in various forms of livelihood programs with emphasis on local participatory mechanism to promote sustainable rural development. In some foreign aid packages, the NGOs were designated as the lead agencies bypassing the government bureaucracy (Goertzen, 1991).

The Philippine Experience

The Cooperative Movement

The historical experience during the last twenty years shows a rather gloomy record of cooperative development efforts. The most ambitious ingredient in the government's promotion campaign for cooperatives was the establishment of the Samahang Nayong (SN) societies serving beneficiaries of the agrarian reform program of 1972.³ The idea is quite simple. All tenants who are agrarian reform beneficiaries are required to become members of the SN before they can be issued a certificate of land transfer (CLT). The SN has two major objectives: (a) to support agrarian reform and (b) to serve as a rural base of the cooperative system (Tirso, 1989). The underlying goal is to substitute the former landlords as suppliers of credit and inputs, and to achieve economies of scale.

The SN has to guarantee that members regularly pay their annual amortization over a 15 years period. Studies, however, show that the SN failed to guarantee these payments and there was not a single case where the SN managed to pay for the liabilities of defaulting members. The only reason why farmers become members of the SN is to qualify for the issuance of the CLT (*ibid.*).⁴ The SN also failed in educating farmers and in mobilizing rural savings. Under the program only 29 rural banks and 56 area marketing cooperatives were established. Recent studies show that two thirds of the 18 000 registered SNs are inactive or dormant (Tirso *op. cit.*).

Some of the major reasons for the failure of the cooperatives (including other types of cooperatives, not just the SNs) are improper organization and officers' mismanagement resulting in low levels of members' participation and a general lack of economic activities (Bonifacio 1989; Quintana 1989).

Despite the failure, cooperatives in various forms continue to be a pillar in the government's programme for rural development. However, there has been a recent change of official attitude towards cooperatives. In 1992 the executive director of the recently formed Cooperative Development Authority pointed out that the number of registered cooperatives had risen to 60 000 but he would be satisfied if 20 000 survive. He emphasized that the future of the cooperative movement lies in being business oriented and able to attract the best minds graduating from college. This is possible, he said, if cooperatives can provide an attractive career in the economic sense (personal interview).

At present, cooperative contract growing is not the mainstream but is far from unique. There are already a number of successful schemes all over the country, such as the papaya livelihood outgrower scheme in Misamis Oriental

---

3 Samahang Nayon is "a body corporate composed primarily of small farmers residing and/or farming within the geographical limits of a village *(barrio)* for the purpose of improving the quality of life of the people" (Quintana 1989).

4 This is a quasi land ownership title which allows the holder to cultivate the land and to use it as collateral, but not to sell it until the full amount is paid to the former owner.

and cooperatively owned vertically integrated feedmills in Cavite and Batangas as well as fruit growing in Quezon province. Export crops such as banana and pineapple(in Mindanao) are partially contracted to small farmers (Hayami, 1990). A similar scheme is proposed for coconuts (Trinidad, 1988). Hayami predicts that as population pressure continues agribusiness will shift from plantation to contract farming.

The Case of the Northern Foods Corporation

The Study Area

The case study area is located in the province of Ilocos Norte at the northwestern tip of the island of Luzon (see map). Bounded in the east by the Cordillera mountain range and by the China Sea in the west, the narrow strip of agricultural land covers an area of 3 400 km² of which approximately 2 000 have slopes above 18%. It is rugged and rocky with an annual rainfall of ca. 2 000 mm. It has two distinct seasons of wet (May to October) and dry (November to April) weather, and is occasionally visited by typhoons during the monsoon period.

At present the area has a projected population of 485 000 and a population density of 142 per km². The population, which is 72% rural, has a growth rate (1,68%) which is below the national average (2,5%). Agricultural employment accounts for 51%, industry for 9% and the remainder is employed in the service sector. The literacy rate is high (97%).

Major crops include fruit, vegetables, root crops and corn. Major commercial crops are tomato, garlic, tobacco and cotton. Of the 22 000 hectares of potentially irrigable area, 97% are irrigated during the rainy season and 21% all year round. In terms of infrastructure the area is considered to have the best network of roads and bridges in the country and telephone, radio communication and telegraph facilities are available in most towns. Although the province has no major agricultural or industrial export product, and is located 500 kms from Manila, the general impression is that people are better off than in many other parts of the country and it has one of the lowest levels of rural poverty in the country (Hayami, 1990).

Map 1. The Philippine Islands and Study Area

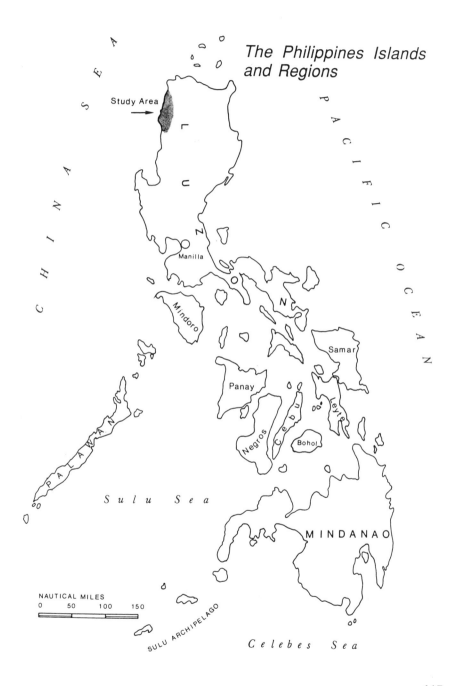

NFC

The Northern Foods Corporation (NFC) is a tomato processing company that began operation in 1984. It was established as an anchor-type[5] processing plant. The important goals of establishing the processing center were multiple. The first goal was to provide alternative incomes and employment to the small farmers in the area. The second purpose was to serve as market to tomato growing farmers. The third objective was to disperse industries and to help technology transfer to the rural countryside. Finally, the reduction of tomato import through substitution and eventually to make possible tomato export as the Philippines has agronomic advantages in tomato production were important considerations.[6]

The initial capitalization was provided by a government financing corporation, Livelihood Corporation (Livecor) but the management of the corporation was assigned to a private firm (Agriman).[7] The local government was involved by allocating a board seat to the provincial governor to represent the interest of the local community. It was envisaged that eventually the

---

5 Anchor-type processing plant refers to the establishment of a processing firm in an area, which will steer farmers to produce agricultural commodity at a commercial scale, in this case, tomato.

6 Comparative advantage in the number of processing days rationale: One of the reasons for establishing the tomato processing in addition to import substitution rationale is the fact that the weather favorable for tomato processing is 134 days for the Philippines compared to only 75-86 days for Taiwan and 85-105 days for California, the two major sources of tomato paste imports (Mateo, 1990).

7 "For the management of NFC, Agriman will be compensated with a management fee of 7%, 6% and 5% of the net sales during the first, second and third year of the company operations respectively. This arrangement was in recognition of its previous efforts in conducting the necessary technical and feasibility studies on tomato processing in the region. In addition, the same group made possible the smooth transfer of tomato technology in both plant and farm operations. This group secured the commitment of the local Del Monte that had the locally available technical work force and marketing capability (available) to NFC. The group also received commitment from Del Monte to purchase tomato paste in the first two years of operations" (Ignacio, 1990).

corporate shares will be sold to the tomato growers either in their individual capacity or as members of the grower's cooperatives.[8]

Since 1987, because of anomalies committed by the private management firm and the high overhead expenses resulting in heavy company losses, the company's management was assumed by government financing corporation Livecor. This action led to the turnaround and partial recovery in the subsequent crop years. During the crop year 1990-91 the company again incurred heavy losses due to overproduction. There were reports of a plan to allow the local cooperatives to take over the ownership of the company.[9] The immediate problem of losses was solved through government emission of new capital.[10]

NFC and Small Farmer Relationship

The region's traditional cash crops are garlic and tobacco. The company has to persuade local farmers to shift their production to tomato instead of the traditional cash crops. Therefore, the company has to show that tomato planting is financially more attractive than alternative cash crops. While the region has a tradition of planting cash crops as an inter-crop to rice, the introduction of a perishable cash crop like tomato demands a tight production schedule and management. It has to be recognized that garlic and tobacco are not as perishable as tomato. The company has virtually to familiarize small

---

8 During my last visit in late 1992, one of the plans was to sell it to the contract-growing cooperatives with a financial package to be partly funded by an aid agency.

9 The author has interviewed the President of the company, operations manager and production manager on separate occasions. They have confirmed in private that plans are being made to package a financial plan which would allow the cooperative growers to take over the company. But local businessmen with strong political connections have shown interest to purchase the plant. When the author visited the area in October 1992, a group of Taiwanese businessmen were visiting to look at the possibility of buying the plant. They were interested of using it not solely for tomato processing but also in processing other fruit crops in the region to increase capacity utilization.

10 In October,1992, President Ramos visited the plant and in a speech to the growers pledged continued government financial support to the project.

farmers with industrial management techniques. The computerized production schedule stipulates the planting schedule of each farm household and the plot of land that has been committed to tomato production and the anticipated harvest schedule. Quality control is very rigorously enforced. During the harvest period, just-in-time (JIT) inventory techniques guide operations to avoid a pile-up of tomato at the processing site as the length of time the tomato is left unprocessed affect the quality of the final product. Another constraint in the scheduling is that the company has to make sure that the tomato production schedule does not overlap with the cropping schedule of the farmers' staple crop (rice).

In 1984, at the beginning of the company's operations in the region, three distinct production arrangements were established: contract growing (individual farmer), corporate farming, and an agricultural loan funded (cooperative membership is required) scheme. Since the 1989-90 season, the company opted to use only the cooperative-based contract growing for reasons to be discussed below.

Contract Growing

Under the contract growing scheme, the individual farmers sign a contract to grow tomato for the NFC. Farmers commit themselves to allocate an area of their farm (maximum 2500 square meters per farmer) to tomatoes. They have to follow the production schedule and adopt the production technology package (seeds, fertilizer and pesticide application, water management) that the NFC technicians have recommended and trained them for. Contract farmers are required to provide labor for farm maintenance until the fruits are harvested. They must sell their entire crop to NFC at predetermined price (price per kilo is negotiated at the start of the season). Selling contracted tomatoes to third parties is prohibited. Farmers are responsible for harvesting and putting the fruits in baskets which are then lined up along the nearest road for scaling (weighing) and transport to the plant. The firm, for its part, supplies all the production inputs and delivers them to the farmers. It is stipulated in the contract that the company collects harvested fruits within 3-5 days after harvest. It is to provide technical assistance to contract growers in the production technology for the fruit. The company has to guarantee a mutually agreed purchase price at the start of the planting season. It has to provide cash support incentive to contract growers (meant to cover irrigation and land preparation expenses).

Farmers who wish to participate in tomato growing are required to undergo training in the cultivation and care of tomato fruit with emphasis in production techniques and quality control. Soil analysis is conducted on the farmer's plot to find out suitability and to test for soil borne diseases. A supervisor with a coverage of thirty (30) hectares is assigned to oversee farms and help tomato growers in the timely and proper application of fertilizer, pesticide and other production activities. These conditions are contained in the contract called the Tomato Marketing Agreement.

Corporate Farms

Under this scheme, the NFC rented land for a six-month period from landowners in the area. The landowners bore no further obligation to the firm except to make the hired land available for the designated period. The land was managed by firm personnel who hired labor on a piece-rate basis to do planting, sowing, irrigation weeding and harvesting. The major problems in this arrangement were the low quality of labor and the shortage of labor during the production period. Because of this type of deficiencies, the corporation suffered three (3) metric tons on-vine spoilage per hectare during harvesting in 1988-89 season.

In a similar case, this predicament was examined by Hayami (1990) in his study of agrarian structure in the Philippines. He claimed that there is no natural advantage of big plantations in crop production because of the problem of supervision of a work place that is geographically spread out like a plantation. There is, on the other hand, a natural advantage for small-holders in crop production because of the requirement of daily caring and monitoring that a small farmer does for his crop. He cited historical examples that plantations were introduced by European companies in Asia in response to European demand for tropical crops in the 19th century. Without sufficient labor during that period, the plantation type of cultivation was the only feasible way of crop cultivation. Today, conditions are the reverse. Labor surplus exists in Asia, or in this case the Philippines, and therefore the smallholder farms are more sensible in this context.

Hayami (1990)also noted the emergence of two categories of cash crop production in the Philippines. One is the traditional plantation type that relies on patron-client relationship with farmers or tenants. The second category is the modern agribusiness type where production is based on modern management relationship. The second type of management relationship has relied more on contract growing or subdividing the area into smaller parcels where results could be easily monitored. The agro-industry being studied belongs to the second category because it is mostly run by professional managers and agronomists who come from different parts of the country and who have no traditional ties with the local community.

Agricultural Loan Funded Farms (Cooperative Membership Required)

This scheme is similar to the contract growing but the contracting party is the cooperative rather than the individual farmer. One criterion for a farmer to participate in this scheme is that he is a member of a cooperative accredited by the company. The supply and marketing contracts are signed between the cooperative and the company. Production loan and other financial assistance are provided by the bank, and not by the firm as in contract growing. However, the farmers continue, under this scheme, to have similar access to company services as free use of sprayers, input delivery, hauling of harvests, and reimbursement of delivery expenses.

Inputs are sold by NFC at cost to the cooperative and the cooperative officials are responsible for distribution, control and documentation of input related transactions with the farmer. Production technology training is provided by the NFC. During harvest, members deliver their produce to the cooperative center for weighing and for accounting purposes in the presence of NFC credit supervisor, scaler, checker and the coop's president or treasurer. The weight records taken at the cooperative center will be the basis for payment. All payments made by the NFC to cooperatives are coursed through the bank. The bank in effect insures that inputs creditors are paid first from the farmer's receipts from the NFC. After that the individual farmers receive their crop payments through their cooperatives.

Current Division of Functions Between the Cooperative and Agro-industry

As farmers' organizations have developed and, what is more important, due to credit incentive provided by the government through the lower interest rate[11] for farmers organized as a cooperative, all growers' contracts are now allocated to the local cooperatives. The company now deals only with the cooperative rather than with individual farmers. Under the present arrangement, the NFC operates under a more decentralized system than earlier (see table 2). Most functions are now delegated to the cooperative. For example, the commitment of land area by individual farmer basis, which was earlier done by the firm is now carried out through the accredited cooperative. Speaking for the farmer-members, cooperatives commit to the firm the land area to be planted with tomato. The grower's contract that stipulates conditions of the tomato growing that include price is signed between the cooperative and the NFC.

After the company has obtained land area commitments sufficient to meet tomato production goals for the year, a round table price negotiation with all cooperatives is conducted between the cooperative representatives and the NFC. The negotiation is aimed to fix the price of tomato for the season based on the specified quality standards of the company. The distance from the processing center is ignored as a pricing factor as the company still assumes the responsibility of hauling the fresh tomato to the processing center. However, if the cooperative growers choose to bring the fruit to the processing plant by themselves, then they will be paid commensurately to the distance of their farm.

The company takes on the task of transporting the tomato from the designated pickup points of each cooperative. The cooperatives carry the assignment of bringing the produce to these pickup points. Nevertheless, the quality of the produce is still an individual farmer's responsibility as sampling for finding out quality is based on each individual farmer's production sample.

---

11 The Land Bank of the Philippines and all rural banks are directed by law to lend to cooperatives at preferential rate 12% compared to the prevailing commercial rate of 16%. In this manner, farmers are encouraged to organize themselves into cooperatives if they want to avail themselves of the lower interest rate

Table 2: Division of Responsibility Between Contract Farm and the Company.

COOPERATIVE	FIRM	BANK(S)	OTHER SECTORS
Land	Guarantee loan	Loan	Fertilizer
Documentation	Assured Market	Financial Intermediation	Seeds
Labour	Training		Baskets
-land preparation	Technical Supervision		Trucks
-planting	Hauling of Tomato		
-weeding			

Cooperative's Role In Inputs Delivery, Credit and Repayment Schemes

Under the new arrangement, several functions that used to be performed by the company have been delegated to the cooperatives. Seeds and fertilizer are no longer sourced from the company but are bought directly from private suppliers. The employees' cooperative of the company competes with private suppliers in bidding to provide the growers' cooperatives with inputs. The system of delivery of these inputs is between the private supplier and the growers' cooperative. For its part, the cooperative distributes the inputs to their members. The timing, type and quantity of these inputs are of course based on the production plan formulated by the company. Seeds are still provided by the company and delivered to the farmers.

It has to be recalled that when the company was newly established these inputs were provided to the contract growers. The inputs were delivered to individual farmers rather than as a group. The costs were then deducted from the value of the product delivered during harvest time. As the farmers became better organized as a cooperative they assumed more responsibility in distribution of inputs, credit, and so forth.

As for credit, the cooperative uses the Tomato Marketing Agreement as collateral to borrow money from the Land Bank or the cooperative rural bank at a preferential lending rate. The author's interview with cooperative officers disclosed that as a matter of practice, the cooperative charged 2-3 percent interest to members to cover administrative costs and to build up the capital base of the cooperative. While this does raise the effective lending rate to the commercial level, the important thing here is that small farmers still benefit since as individuals they do not have access to the banking institutions. Without this arrangement they would be compelled to borrow from the informal sector at rates that could go up to 240 per cent annually.

As a cooperative, the farmers are collectively liable for the repayment of the credit of individual members. So there is social and legal pressure that each member who borrowed money in the name of the cooperative should pay back their loans on time. In addition, the company payments to farmers for fruits are coursed through the bank. Input suppliers and other creditors have prior claim to this money and input loans are deducted before the balance is remitted to the individual farmer or cooperative. Repayment rates are very high, varying between 86 and 97 percent in the years 1989/90 to 91/92 (NFC Annual Evaluation Survey, various years).

Productivity Schemes

In the preceding years, productivity was encouraged by introducing a differentiated pricing system. Farmers were paid a higher price for producing above 30 tons per hectare. In other words, for the first 30 tons the farmer was paid PPH 0.30 per kilo and for the succeeding tonnage PPH 0.50/kg. The problem was that it was difficult to monitor whether the tomato produce above this level came from the same plot of land or was taken from other farmers to take advantage of the higher price. Despite this incentive, it took five years before the farmers could raise their average productivity to this level.

This was later changed to allow only those farmers who achieved certain levels of productivity to participate in the program. Those areas that could not reach the level of productivity required were excluded in the subsequent planting season. However, the most significant determining factor is the economic one. As financing is now shouldered by the contracting cooperative, the level of productivity determines the profitability of tomato growing for farmers. Pricing is identical for tomato of similar quality whatever their geographical location. Since prices are set at the beginning of the planting season, the profitability of tomato growing is primarily decided by the level of productivity. Conditions for continued participation remain that only those farmers who have a track record of producing between 30-40 tons per hectare shall participate in contract growing.

Employment Impact

The direct employment impact is easy to estimate but the indirect impact is problematic. The direct employment broadly refers to the labor employment generated in the processing plant, and the direct on-farm employment because of their cultivation of tomato. The indirect employment can include ancillary services such as hauler trucks that transport the harvested tomato. The basket makers and the input suppliers like the fertilizer and pesticide firms also belong to this category. For purposes of this essay it is sufficient to refer to direct employment effects, which are mainly the processing plant employment and the farmers directly engaged in the production of tomato.

The company itself estimated the direct farm employment through the number of households contracted by the company. Since the company demands a fresh tomato fruit tonnage of between 53,000 - 67,000 metric tons for one season, this requires a total farm area of 1,250-1,500 hectares (assuming a productivity level of 42 tons/ha.). At an average of 0.2 hectare per farm household, the projected total farm households to participate in the program would be 6,250-7,500 contract growers. If there are only three adult workers per family, this means a seasonal employment of 18,750 to 22,500 persons.

The experience of the past several years does not seem to support this optimistic projection of the number of farmers engaged in tomato growing. The number of farmers cultivating tomato for the company in 1987[12] is almost the same level as of the 1991-92 planting season that involved 2,500 farmers (or seasonally employed household members of 7,500). The peak level of operation in 1989-90 has not been approximated ever since.

There were only three planting seasons in the past nine years that the firm could plant above the 1,000 hectares (see Table 3.). During the last two years the company was only able to plant above 600 hectares compared to 1,400

---

[12] The third year is used as a base year because according to the studies on the subject, one needs at least 2-3 years to approach normal operations.

hectares in the 1989-90 season. Productivity increases compensated for the reduction in hectares. The total production level is below the rated capacity utilization of the company.

TABLE 3: NFC - Data on Production 1984 - 1992

Crop Year	Area (ha)	Yield (tons/ha)	No. of Farmers	Villages Covered
1984-85	243	15,9	813	56
1985-86	694	19,0	2,596	142
1986-87	812	18,4	5,853	284
1987-88	356	19,9	2,655	163
1988-89	886	32,9	6,166	324
1989-90	1,498	39,5	8,514	328
1990-91	1,103	34,8	4,457	229
1992-93	644	n.a.	2,512	n.a.

Source: NFC Reports, various years.

One disadvantage of using this type of estimate is that tomato growing involve farmers and cooperatives for only part of the cropping year. One way out of this dilemma of estimating employment is to use the normative concept of man-days[13] for the given amount of agricultural activity. Based on the standard used by the Provincial Agriculturist's Office in the area, the average employment of tomato growing per hectare is 147 man-days. Based on the normative employment rate of tomato production, our own estimates show that direct on-farm employment has declined to 94,000 man-days for the last season from the peak employment of 174,000 man-days in 1988-89. The reduction in the area cultivated with tomato could largely explain this declined. The company is restricting the cultivation of tomato to areas with high productivity. The huge losses that the company suffered in the 1989-90 were due to overproduction, therefore the reluctance to increase cultivation

---

13 One man-day is equivalent to 8 adult working hours. A minor or child would be credited with equivalent 1/2 man-day for 8 working hours (see Lipton,1977).

area. The company is still saddled with large tomato paste inventory accumulated from past harvests. The reduction of production has also led to the decline of personnel employed in the processing plant as part of the rationalization plan to cut losses.

Table 4: Direct Employment a)

Crop Year	87/88	88/89	89/90	90/91	91/92	92/93
Processing Plant b) (Man-days)	53,500	56,250	62,750	59,250	47,500	37,000
On-Farm Employment c) (Man-days)	199,360	496,160	838,320	617,120	381,360	

Source: NFC Agri-production and Extension Unit Farm Plan, Provincial Agriculturist's Office Field Reports, Author's own estimates

   a. We disregard the first three years because this is considered the "normalization" period of agro-industries according to Glover (1990).
   b. There is difficulty of expressing the employment rate in a common unit of measurements because obviously on-farm employment and other ancillary services like transport are not a year round occupations. However, this is not the case for processing plant employment that is to large degree an eight-hour day work throughout the year.
   c. According to the NFC estimates employment is roughly estimated at three adults employed for every participating farmer. However this is a rough measure because of the different farm sizes of the tomato growers. We therefore choose to use the standard estimate of the Department of Agriculture that is based on the normative concept of the number of man-days of labor input per hectare production - 147 man-days and 26 animal-days.

Import Substitution Rationale

The significance of this agro-processing industry lies in the fact that the Philippines, despite its favorable agronomic conditions for tomato production, imported a total of 13,491 metric tons of tomato paste costing the country 9.8 million US dollars in 1988. This has declined with total tomato paste imports only valued at USD 1.2 million as of 1990.[14] The NFC as major supplier of tomato paste in the country claims credit for the decline of paste imports and the savings of foreign exchange.

---

14 NFC Annual Report, 1991.

Technology

The firm has introduced a new technology package in the region to meet the demand of tomato growing. It adopted several strategies to address the issue. One was to train farmers who wanted to participate in the program in the production of the crop. While the local farmers have long experience in cash crop production like garlic and tobacco, they did not have the production knowledge for a perishable commodity like tomato. They were taught the whole process of planting the tomato. The planting schedule must be strictly observed and the application of fertilizer and pesticide too. During harvest, NFC technicians guide the farmers with quality control techniques.

As far as one could gather from interviews with both company officials and cooperative representatives, the technology package has been effective in making the small farmers observe modern ways of tomato growing and in raising productivity to acceptable levels. If at all, it is the company that could not cope with the demands as the annual evaluation report showed that some farmers were complaining about the delay in the hauling of their crops.[15]

Impact On Farmers' Income

One way of looking at the impact of agro-industries on the farmers' income would be to estimate the direct payment of the NFC to the farmers. These payments have increased from 4 million PPh in 1987/88 to almost 47 million PPh in 1990/91 (NFC Annual Report, various years). This information, however, is obviously insufficient as we have to factor in the cost structure of tomato cultivation and as we have to compare the income that could be obtained under different organizational relationships. We are interested in making a comparison of the earnings that individual contract growing could earn in contrast with cooperative contract growing.

The individual contract grower earns less than the cooperative-based contract grower (Table 6). The main reason for this is the higher productivity of cooperative-based contract growing as compared to individual contract growers. The productivity level of cooperative growers during the last season

---

15 In some studies (Glover,1990; Stanford,1990) referring to Latin American cases, the delay in hauling of tomato for example is deliberate effort to allow evaporation to set in and thus decreasing the weight of tomato and hence lower the price paid to the farmer.

appears to have declined but it is still much higher. Since the adoption of the policy of allowing only cooperative growers in 1989-90, the average productivity levels of growers are higher than in the previous years.

In the author's interview with some cooperative leaders, they were asked why they preferred to plant tomato rather than garlic, a competing cash crop in the region. The most common reply given is the price stability of tomato in the sense that price is fixed at the beginning of the season, while the price of garlic is wildly fluctuating. The farmers have experienced that the price of garlic sometimes plunged to levels barely able to compensate for their production costs. They find planting other cash crops too risky.

Farmers' Access to Credit

The participation of farmers in the tomato production has immensely improved their access to formal sources of credit. The formal requirements to borrow money from a bank are too complicated for an ordinary farmer to comply with without the assistance of the company. The NFC gives various forms of assistance to cooperatives in easing their loan application. It helps the cooperatives in preparing the loan documentation and gives training to cooperative officers in basic accounting methods. It also uses its good offices to hasten processing of the loan.

The initial access of farmers to the formal banking institution through the Tomato Marketing Agreement (TMA) helps them establish a track record with the credit institution. This is no mean achievement for small farmers for this gives them an opportunity for other things as well. The credibility that the farmers have established in the production of tomato helped them in expediting their application for production loan in their staple crop - rice. On the other hand, the banks have the assurance that if the farmers do not do well in rice they have a second chance of recovering the loan in the tomato production or vice-versa.

The payment scheme is so designed that the bank and other creditors have the right to be paid first from the commodity payment to farmers. This gives assurance to the bank that payment will be forthcoming. The farmers' loan with the bank is a joint liability with the cooperative to which the farmer is a member. Therefore social pressure comes into play in making sure that loans are repaid. The record of repayment attests to the effectiveness of this model.

Table 5: Northern Foods Corporation

Cost-Benefit Analysis
Coop Farms versus Contract Growing Farms (1989-90 Cropping Season)

I. NFC Contract Growing Costs		
Cash Support to Farmers		3,000
NFC's Inputs Subsidy		9,000
Seeds	850	
Fertilizer	3,000	
Pesticide	2,000	
Fungicide	2,500	
Irrigation	650	
Purchase Cost		9,890
Average Yield (MT)	31.72 MT	
Purchase Price		
First 30 kgs.	PPH 0.30	
Over 30 kgs.	0.50	
Total NFC Cost/kilo	0.59	
Farmers' Revenue		21,860
Expenses		13,000
FARMER'S NET INCOME		8,860
II. Coopertive Farm Costs (Per Hectare)		
NFC Purchase Price/kilo	PPH 1.10	
Average Yield (MT)	61.32 MT	
Farmers Revenue		67,452
Expenses		12,200
Seeds	850	
Fertilizer	3,000	
Pesticide	2,000	
Fungicide	2,500	
Hired Labour and Land Preparation	3,000	
Irrigation	650	
Management Fee plus Loan Interest	200	
FARMER'S NET INCOME		55,252

Source: Ignacio (1990)

This type of arrangement does not only benefit the contract-farmer. It is equally beneficial to the firm. Earlier, the company gave credit directly to farmers' production inputs to be checked off from the farmers' commodity payment at the end of the season. Now several functions are delegated to other institutions. The bank provides the credit and the private input supplier or cooperative furnish the inputs. This also saves administrative costs to the company. More important, this allows an opportunity for a multidimensional local economy as the various institutions play their role in the economy.

Concluding Remarks

In the context of this specific experience, we would now address the following research issues and make a comparison with the experience of similar agro-industries found in various studies reviewed. First we look at the motivations of the partners in entering the contract farm arrangement. According to earlier studies on agro-industries in several countries, the possible motivation of both the growers and the agro-processing industries is suggested by examining the specific problems of each individual institution. Based on this, one could delineate the advantages that each participant derives by entering into the contract growing relationship. It was postulated that the system can be mutually beneficial for different reasons.

Firms entering into the contract growing relationship can derive advantages because they have a degree of control in the production process without additional investment in land. They can refrain from hiring production labor or manage large scale farming operations that may strain the managerial and technical expertise of a primarily industrial firm. In addition, they can avoid the sensitive issue of landownership and possible conflict over labor relations.

The case studied confirms this hypothesis. The cost involved in land acquisition would have been tremendous. The dislocation that would have arisen to acquire settled land would have been socially dysfunctional. Further cost saving is derived by delegating administrative and supervision costs to the cooperative. The financing cost of production is transferred to the contract grower and partly to the taxpayer. The land bank and rural banks administer the subsidy system by lending to the contract growing cooperative at a subsidized rate of 12% per cent instead of the prevailing commercial rate of 16%.

The advantages and efficiency of smallholder production for crops that require intensive labor and careful attention over the production methods employed by plantations are well documented in previous studies (Glover,

1990). This view was recently substantiated in a study (Hayami, 1990) of agrarian structure in the Philippines that included established agro-industries like Dole and Del Monte. Hayami's study confirmed the view that large plantation is an inefficient mode of producing cash crops except in instances where economies of scale for the specific infrastructure like irrigation or pest management could be derived. The study revealed that even big plantations clone the advantages of a small farm by subdividing their land into smaller plots for better supervision.

Our own study reveals that where quality is an important parameter for accepting the crop, smallholder production is an obvious advantage. A comparison of productivity figures showed clearly the higher productivity of smallholder production (both cooperative based and individual) over the corporate farms using hired labor. The recognition of this fact led the company to abandon the corporate run farms and shifted to using only cooperative-based smallholder contract growing since 1990.

Yet another advantage mentioned by Glover is that local firms could pay lower wages than foreign ones without bringing in the political dimension of foreign exploitation. They can pay workers less and deal more harshly with unions without provoking social conflict. In our study, this cannot be affirmed unequivocally because in-plant wages are set according to existing laws and compliance is apparently observed. As to farm labor, this is always set by prevailing labor market conditions and considering that there are laws penalizing non-observance of minimum wages, it is extremely difficult to elicit truthful answers to questions on this issue. Since the company has adopted a cooperative-based smallholding as unit for production and uses mainly household labor, this issue is not crucial anymore.

The assertion that local firms can get local government to provide credit easier is also confirmed in the study. The incentives to firms to locate their activity in the region normally include provision of tax holidays and access to local credit market. The case showed that cheap credit to small farmers is indeed made available by formal credit institutions through government subsidy. The agro-industry firm concerned directly benefitted from this cheap credit because it lessened their cost of operations and the price for the commodity is made more competitive. On the other hand, small farmers without any credit facility from the formal banking institution or guarantee from agro-industry would become victimized by the informal credit market that charges usurious interests rate. Government policy is clearly responsible for this benefit to the small farmers. It should be added that the small farmers organized as cooperatives have themselves become a pressure group on the government to maintain the cheap credit even as the government itself has become reluctant to maintain the policy due to budgetary and other economic constraints.

The access of small farmers to credit is eased by participation in the production agreement with the agro-industry. It does not require additional resources other than the existing land and the available household labor. The case mentioned is particularly critical because it gives farmers access to formal credits even for their staple crops.

It is often asserted that the contract growing provides an opportunity to form an alliance with local business interests to defend the multinationals' interest on certain issues (Glover, *op cit.*). In this specific case, the company is locally owned and managed so this hypothesis cannot be tested. It has to be mentioned that there was a marketing agreement that during the first three years the multinational food giant Del Monte would buy the processed product and thus providing it with a ready market.

On the other hand, the small farmers see contract growing as the answer to some traditional problems. The risks of adopting new technologies are minimized by contract growing. In our study, the risks to smallholders were overcome through the provision by the company of the smallholder support services such as training, technical assistance during the production period, credit, inputs, hauling facilities and an assured market.

The ratio of extension workers to the number of farmers to be supervised is often incredibly low in developing countries (c.f. Holmén 1991). The proportion, in this case, of one extension worker per approximately 150 farmers (thirty hectares of land) is unthinkable in the government extension service. Another important dimension to this issue is the way in which extension works in the developing world. Generally, its organization does not give weight to accountability such as if the farmer failed to produce according to specified level of productivity, the extension worker does not lose his job and is protected by civil service rules on job tenure. The accountability dimension in the contract grower relationship is immediate. The failure to produce the required quantity and quality of the product has immediate effect on the operations of the company (or worse, go bankrupt) and therefore the very livelihood of the extension worker. This serves as incentive for good quality extension work.

The agro-industry provides the channels for access to markets, which otherwise are not available to the small farmers. The NFC markets tomato paste to large and medium-sized domestic and multinational (Del Monte) food processors. This market niche is obviously not accessible to small farmers on the individual basis. In the past, these food processing industries imported tomato paste from abroad to satisfy their demand.

The employment effects discussed earlier in the essay have significant employment impact. The size of its employment in terms of contract growers and other ancillary may be a disadvantage since politicians may start interfering in the operation to use it as a source of patronage for their political followers since the processing plant is government-owned. After a transition, the ideal situation would be to turn it over to the contract growing cooperatives. In general, therefore, the contract growing in the region has been mutually beneficial to contract growing cooperatives and the company involved.

References

Austin J (1981): *Agroindustrial Project Analysis*. Baltimore, Md., John Hopkins University Press.

Bonifacio M (1989): "Some Sociological Insights on Cooperative Development" in *State of Cooperative Development in the Philippines*. Quezon City: Cooperative Foundation Philippines, Inc.

Chapman K, Walker D (1987): *Industrial Location*. Oxford: Basil Blackwell.

Friedmann J, Weaver C (1979): *Territory and Function: The Evolution of Regional Planning*. London: Edward Arnold Publishers.

Glover D (1983): *Contract Farming and the Transnationals*. Unpublished Ph.D. dissertation (Department of Political Economy, University of Toronto).

Glover D, Klusterer K (1990): *Small Farmers, Big Business*. London: MacMillan Press.

Goertzen D (1991): "Agents for Change," *Far Eastern Economic Review*, August 8,1991, pp.20-21.

Goldberg R, MacGinity R (eds.) (1979): *Agribusiness Management for Developing Countries*. Cambridge, Massachusetts: Harper & Row Publishers.

Goldsmith A (1985): "The Private Sector and Rural Development: Can Agribusiness Help Small Farmers?," *World Development* 13 (10/11): 1125-1138.

Hayami, Yujiro, et. al., 1978, *Anatomy of a Peasant Economy: A Rice Village in the Philippines*. Los Banos: International Rice Research Institute.

Hirschman AO (1958): *The Strategy of Economic Development*. New Haven: Yale University Press.

Ho S (1979): "Decentralized Industrialization and Rural Development: Evidence from Taiwan," *Economic Development and Cultural Change*.

Holmén H (1991): *Building Organizations for Rural Development. State and Cooperatives in Egypt*. Lund, Lund University Press

International Labour Organization (1974): *Sharing in Development: A Programme of Employment Equity and Growth for the Philippines*. Geneva, ILO.

Ignacio R (1990): *A Case Study of Northern Foods Corporation*. Metro-Manila, Asian Institute for Management(mimeograph).

Lappe F, Collins J (1977): *Food First: Beyond the Myth of Scarcity*. Boston, Houghton Mifflin.

Lipton M, Connell J (1977): *Assessing Labour Situations in Developing Countries*. Delhi: Oxford University Press.

Lo F-C, Salih K (1978): "Growth Poles and Regional Policy in Open Dualistic Economies: Western Theory and Asian Reality" in *Growth Pole Strategy and Regional Development Policy*. UNCRD, Pergamon Press, New York.

Mateo F (1990): *Shaping the Future of the Vegetable Processing Industry*. Paper presented to the symposium on "The Philippine Vegetable Processing Industry: Status, Problems and Prospects" University of the Philippines at Los Banos, October 24, 1990.

Northern Foods Corporation, *Annual Reports*, various years. Metro Manila: Northern Foods Corporation.

Ofreneo R E (1981): *Capitalism in Philippine Agriculture*. Quezon City, Foundation for Nationalist Studies.

Pantasen A (1989): *Agro-industry and Self-reliance Strategies in Thailand*. Seminar Paper in Conference "Rural Southeast Asia in Transition" held in Lund, Sept.28-October 1,1989 (mimeo.).

Philippine Agribusiness Factbook, 1991. Metro Manila, Center for Research and Communication.

Philippine Government (1989): *Philippine Development Report*, Manila, Government Printers.

Philippine Government (1990): "Countryside Agro-Industrial Development Strategy," *Philippine Development*, 17(1): 10-14, Jan.-February, 1990

Quintana V (1989): "Financing and Managing Cooperative: Issues and Problems and Recommendations," in *State of Cooperative Development in the Philippines*. Quezon City, Cooperative Foundation Philippines, Inc.

Santika A (1991): *The Impact of Agro-Industries in Indonesia*. Unpublished Ph.D. dissertation at the Department of Resource Development, Michigan State University.

Saith A (1991): "Asian Rural Industrialization Context, Features, Strategies," in Jan Bremen (Ed.): *Rural Transformation in Asia*. Oxford: Oxford University Press.

Stanford ML (1990): *International Agribusiness and the Small Farmers: Cantaloupes, Competition, and Caciques in Michoacan, Mexico*. Unpublished Ph.D. dissertation at the University of Florida.

Timmer P (1991) *The Role of Agricultural Exports in Development*. New York, Cornell University Press.

Tirso C (1989): "Government Policies and Programs on Philippine Cooperatives," in *State of Cooperative Development in the Philippines*. Quezon City: Cooperative Foundation Philippines, Inc.

Valdes A (1991): "The Role of Agricultural Exports in Development," in Peter Timmer (Ed.): *Agriculture and the State*. New York, Cornell University Press

White SP (1983): *Agro-Industries in Ghana: An Examination of their Efficacy in Rural Development*. Unpublished Ph.D. dissertation at UCLA.

Post Scriptum

For several decades, high expectations have been placed on local organizations as 'development vehicles' in poor countries. In the early years of LO promotion, state administered development of, for example, co-operative organizations was the generally accepted model for organization building in the rural areas. Development strategies for the majority of poor countries in the 1950's - 1970's advocated fast industrial development and modernization and placed less emphasis on agricultural/rural development. In many cases governments deliberately taxed the agricultural sector heavily in order to finance urban/industrial growth. At the time when these 'anti-rural power structures' were created, governments often made comprehensive proclamations about the potential development force embedded in co-operative organizations. In retrospect, one may wonder whether the relatively inexpensive (from a government resource allocation point of view) creation of centrally controlled organizations in rural areas was a way of distracting attention from the pressing, but more costly, needs for development of rural infrastructure and agricultural research and modernization. At the time, governments in the Third World did not face any severe criticism against their policies. On the contrary, they were supported by western donor agencies and many over-zealous social reformists and like-minded urban intellectuals who often, romantically, referred to the traditional co-operative movement.

Today, the calls for LOs/NGOs are perhaps stronger than ever. This can, as has been discussed in this anthology, hardly be explained by positive experiences of past performance of LOs. More likely, it is the result of changing conditions in the Third World and of the experience gained from earlier development efforts. A more critical view on the role of the state in Third World development has emerged. State-led industrial growth financed partly by discriminating agricultural/rural policies is no longer seen as the key to economic progress.[1] Although one cannot expect the "urban bias" in development thinking to disappear overnight, there seems to be a growing consensus about the need for a more balanced growth. Such an awareness is partly the result of environmental degradation and resource depletion taking

---

1 However, Schultz (1993:17) reminds us that is is "regrettable but true that this doctrine is still supported by some donor agencies and rationalized by some economists in high-income countries.

place in many Third World countries. Increasing population pressure in combination with a neglect of rural and agricultural development has often forced poor people to cultivate their land in a non-sustainable manner and/or to expand into marginal and hazard-prone areas where the land resource is rapidly deteriorating. The strong link between poverty and environmental degradation is today clear.

The presently increasing support for LOs/NGOs then, has a rationale that is, at least partly, different from the older waves of support. Having observed the difficulties in reaching the poorest segments in society through organizational efforts administered by government or government-controlled organizations, an emphasis on *non*-governmental organizations is now made. But will it be enough to exclude government influence? Are todays' LOs/NGOs - often created from organizational concepts drawn up by non-rural, rich-world mother organizations - the development vehicles of tomorrow? If reaching the poor is on the top of the agenda and if this objective is seen as a part of a strategy to find forms for environmental protection, important questions concerning the organizational forms of such organizations remain to be solved.

Older forms of rural LOs have mainly been organizations for farmers. In the 1950's and 1960's small-scale farmers constituted the majority of the poor in developing countries. This picture is rapidly changing in many countries. In large parts of the Third World, rural economies and rural labour markets have profoundly changed and diversified since 'organization-building for development' first took off some decades ago. The small farmer is no longer the typical rural dweller and the poor are, increasingly, the landless.

> "An increasing proportion of people in *severe* poverty ... derive their scanty livelihoods mainly from rural employment, not from farming. In Bangladesh, Eastern India and Java, such 'landless and near-landless labourers' are already a majority of the severly poor; in many other places, including Kenya, they soon will be" (Lipton 1989:68)

The implication of these socio-economic changes, together with the need for environmental protection, accentuates the need to develop new forms of local organizations. Such forms must take into consideration the diversity of rural environments in the Third World. More than ever, location-specific conditions need to be understood and reckoned with when the new local organizations are erected.

In the theoretical debate about development, 'Grand Theory' has long been 'out'. Let it not survive in practical implementation of development projects! The so common polarization between development debaters, believing in one approach or another, and their inability to leave their trenches have crippled development practice - not least when it comes to organization building. Paraphrasing Chambers (1984) it is commonly the case that little attention has been paid to the psychology and sociology of ignorance, prejudice and the selective use of evidence in analyzing local organizations. Chambers (1984:362), in relation to green revolution technology, notes the "polarization between those who have taken views which are positive and optimistic, and those whose views have been negative and pessimistic" (see also Rigg 1989; Pierce 1990). Chambers (1987) also points to the inability of 'negative academics' and 'positive practitioners' to arrive at a common view on potentials and effects of development projects and programmes. It can therefore be hoped that now, when new organizational forms are to emerge, they will be permitted to develop according to local needs, preconditions and realities. If representatives of the rapidly expanding western-based NGOs find it convenient to try to squeeze southern local organizations into their own ready made organizational costumes and to control them from outside/above, these organizations will once again be given a role far below their potential.

The present enthusiasm about NGOs must be balanced by thorough empirical investigation of their efficiency in quantitative as well as qualitative terms. Such inquiries have to date been sadly neglected (Riddell, 1990).

On the whole, there is still confusion about what a local organization is and we need to increase our knowledge about their numbers, forms, effects and impacts locally as well as nationally. This calls for a comprehensive inventory of existing and possibly emerging LOs/southern NGOs. Such an inventory seems to be needed, not least in the case of the commonly referred to "environmental NGOs" which are believed being able to solve a variety of severe problems in a number of distinct physical settings all over the Third World.

References

Chambers R (1984): Beyond the Green Revolution: a selective essay. In Bayliss-Smith and Wanmali (Eds.): *Understanding Green Revolutions*. Cambridge University Press, Cambridge. pp 362-379.

Chambers R (1987): *Rural Development - Putting the Last First.* Longman, New York.

Schultz TW (1993): *The Economics of Being Poor.* Blackwell, Oxford UK, Cambridge USA.

Lipton M (1989): *New Seeds and Poor People.* The Johns Hopkins University Press, Baltimore.

Rigg JD (1989): The new rice technology and agrarian change: guilt by association? *Progress in Human Geography* 13 (3), pp374-399.

Riddel R (1990): *Judging Success - Evaluating NGO Approaches to Alleviate Poverty in Developing Countries.* ODI Working Paper 37, Overseas Development Institute, London.

Pierce JT (1990): *The Food Resource.* Longman, Harlow GB.

About the Authors

Neelambar Hatti is presently Associate Professor at the Department of Economic History, Lund University, formerly Professor and Director of IMPART Centre, Hyderabad, India.

Hans Holmén is Lecturer at the Department of Social and Economic Geography, Lund University. He has worked as volunteer for a relief-NGO in Jordan and conducted research on rural co-operatives in Africa and Egypt.

Magnus Jirström, B.Sc. in economics, is presently Ph.D-student at the Department of Social and Economic Geography, Lund University. He has conducted research on co-operatives and local organizations in Zimbabwe and Malaysia.

Esteban Pagaran, M.A. in regional planning, is presently Ph.D-student at the Department of Social and Economic Geography, Lund University. He has worked for the UN/ILO in southern Africa and conducted research on co-operatives and local organizations in the Philippines.

Franz-Michael Rundquist is Associate Professor at the Department of Social and Economic Geography, Lund University. He has conducted research on co-operatives and rural development in India and Africa.

LUND STUDIES IN GEOGRAPHY

For sale at Lund University Press, Box 141, 221 00 Lund, Sweden
Adress to authors and for exchange: Department of Geography,
Sölvegatan 13, S-223 62 Lund, Sweden

Series B. Human Geography

1. *Bergsten, K.E. (1949)* A Methodological Study of an Ancient Hinterland. The Iron Factory c Finspång, Sweden.
2. *Kant, E. (1950)* Quelques problèmes concernant la représentation de la densité des habitatio rurales. Examples pris en Estonie.
3. Studies in Rural-urban Interaction. (1951) *Kant, E.:* Umland Studies and Sector Analysis. - *Godlund, S.:* Bus Services, Hinterlands, and the Location of Urban Settlements in Sweden, specially in Scania. - *Bergsten, K.E.:* Variability in Intensity of Urban Fields as illustrated b Birth-places. - *Hägerstrand, T.:* Migration and the Growth of Culture Regions.
4. *Hägerstrand, T. (1952)* The Propagation of Innovation Waves.
5. *Lägnert, F. (1952)* The Electorate in the Country Districts of Scania 1911-1948.
6. *Godlund, S. (1952)* Ein Innovationsverlauf in Europa, dargestellt in einer vorläufigen Untersuchung über die Ausbreitung der Eisenbahninnovation. (Resume: Un processus d'innovation en Europe, exposé par une recherche préliminaire sur la propagation des innovations des chemins de fer).
7. *Pålsson, E. (1953)* Gymnasiums and Communications in Southern Götaland.
8. *Nordström, O. (1953)* Die Beziehungen zwischen Hüttenwerken und ihrem Umland in Sudschweden von 1750-1900.
9. *Wendel, B. (1953)* A Migration Schema. Theories and Observations.
10. *Nordström, O. (1953)* Verteilung der Altersklassen und Geschlechter in den verschiedener Gesellscahftsgruppen im südöstlichen Schweden von 1800-1910.
11. *Ajo, R. (1953)* Contributions to Social Physics. A Programme Sketch with Special Regard National Planning.
12. *Hannerberg, D. (1955)* Die älteren Skandinavischen Ackermasse. Ein Versuch zu einer zusammenfassenden Theorie.
13. Migration in Sweden. A Symposium. Edited by *Hannerberg, D., Hägerstrand, T.* and *Odeving, B. (1957).*
14. *Kulldorff, G. (1955)* Migration Probabilities.
15. *Ajo, R. (1955)* An Analysis of Automobile Frequencies in a Human Geographic Continuu
16. *Ahlberg, G. (1956)* Population Trends and Urbanization in Sweden 1911-1950.

17. *Godlund, S. (1956)* Bus Service in Sweden.
18. *Godlund, S. (1956)* The Function and Growth of Bus Traffic within the Sphere of Urban Influence.
19. *Nordström, O. (1958)* Pendelwanderungen in die Industriorte in Südschweden 1750-1955. Eine Studie über die Möglichkeiten der Fabriken die Reservarbeitskraft des Umlandes auszunutzen.
20. *Hannerberg, D. (1960)* Schonische Bolskiften.
21. *Godlund, S. (1961)* Population, Regional Hospitals, Transport Facilities, and Regions. Planning the Location of Regional Hospitals in Sweden.
22. *Eldblom, L. (1962)* Quelques points de vue comparatifs sur les problèmes d'irrigation dans les trois oasis libyennes de Brâk, Ghadamès et particulièrement Mourzouk.
23. *Törnqvist, G. (1962)* Transport Costs as a Location Factor for Manufacturing Industry.
24. Proceedings of the IGU Symposium in Urban Geography, Lund 1960. Edited by *Norborg, K. (1962)*.
25. *Grytzell, K.G. (1963)* The Demarcation of Comparable City Areas by Means of Population Density.
26. *Morrill, R. (1965)* Migration and the Spread and Growth of Urban Settlement.
27. *Pred, A. (1967)* Behaviour and Location. Foundations for a Geographic and Dynamic Location Theory. Part I.
28. *Pred, A. (1969)* Behaviour and Location. Foundations for a Geographic and Dynamic Location Theory. Part II.
29. *Brown, L.A. (1968)* Diffusion Dynamics. A Review and Revision of the Quantitative Theory of the Spatial Diffusion of Innovation.
30. *Törnqvist, G. (1968)* Flows of Information and the Location of Economic Activities.
31. *Illeris, S.* and *Pedersen, P.O. (1968)* Central Places and Functional Regions in Denmark. Factor Analysis of Telephone Traffic.
32. *Eighmy, T.H. (1968)* Problems of Census Interpretation in Developing Countries: The Western Nigeria Case.
33. *Grytzell, K.G. (1969)* County of London. Population Changes 1801-1901.
34. *Grytzell, K.G. (1970)* Methods for Demarcation of Cities Compared.
35. *Törnqvist, G. (1970)* Contact Systems and Regional Development.
36. *Kant, E. (1970)* Über die ersten absoluten Punktkarten der Bevölkerungsverteilung. Bemerkungen zur Geschichte der thematischen Kartographie.
37. Information Systems for Regional Development - A Seminar. General Papers. Edited by *Hägerstrand, T.* and *Kuklinski, A.R. (1971)*
38. *Pred, A.* and *Törnqvist, G. (1973)* System of Cities and Information Flows.
39. *Engström, M.G.* and *Sahlberg, B. (1973)* Travel Demand, Transport Systems and Regional Development.
40. *Blazek, B., Petz, J., Stoklasa, J. (1974)* Anthropo-ecological decision-making. On the analysis of implicit assumptions intervening between biological and economic approaches.

41. *Naiduayah, N. (✝) (1975)* Spatial Aspects of Social Change. A Social Geography of the Kikuyu.
42. *Gould, P. (1975)* People in Information Space: The Mental Maps and Information Surfaces of Sweden.
43. *Öberg, S. (1976)* Methods of Describing Physical Access to Supply Points.
44. *Lenntorp, B. (1976)* Paths in Space-time Environments. A Time-geographic Study of Movement Possibilities of Individuals.
45. *Törnqvist, G. (1979)* On Fragmentation and Coherence in Regional Research.
46. *Morrill, R. (1979)* On the Spatial Organization of the Landscape.
47. *Mårtensson, S. (1979)* On the Formation of Biographies in Space-time Environments.
48. Space and Time in Geography: Essays Dedicated to Torsten Hägerstrand. Edited by *Pred, A. (1981)*.
49. *Carlstein, T. (1982)* Time Resources, Society and Ecology: On the Capacity for Human Interaction in Space and Time in Preindustrial Societies.
50. Creativity and Context. A Seminar Report. Edited by *Buttimer, A. (1983)*.
51. *Sporrek, A. (1985)* Food Marketing and Urban Growth in Dar Es Salaam.
52. *Hägerstrand, T.* and *Buttimer, A. (eds.) (1988)* Geographers of Norden. Reflections on Career Experiences.
53. *Gyllström, B.* and *Rundquist, F-M. (eds.) (1989)* State, Cooperatives and Rural Change.
54. *Buttimer, A. (1990)* The Wake of Erasmus.
55. *Friberg, T. (1993)* Everyday Life: Women's Adaptive Strategies in Time and Space.
56. *Holmén, H.* and *Jirström, M. (Eds.) (1994)* Ground Level Development: NGOs, Co-operatives and Local Organizations in the Third World.